KINDNESS & SALT

Recipes for
THE CARE & FEEDING
OF
YOUR FRIENDS & NEIGHBORS

RYAN ANGULO & DOUG CROWELL

Photographs by Liz Barclay • *Illustrations by Owen Brozman*

GRAND CENTRAL
Life&Style
NEW YORK • BOSTON

Grand Central Life & Style
Hachette Book Group
1290 Avenue of the Americas, New York, NY 10104
grandcentrallifeandstyle.com
twitter.com/grandcentralpub

First Edition: November 2018

Grand Central Life & Style is an imprint of Grand Central Publishing. The Grand Central Life & Style
name and logo are trademarks of Hachette Book Group, Inc.

The publisher is not responsible for websites (or their content) that are not owned by the publisher.

The Hachette Speakers Bureau provides a wide range of authors for speaking events.
To find out more, go to www.hachettespeakersbureau.com or call (866) 376-6591.

Library of Congress Cataloging-in-Publication Data
Names: Angulo, Ryan, author. | Crowell, Doug, author.
Title: Kindness & salt : recipes for the care and feeding of your friends and
neighbors / Ryan Angulo, Doug Crowell.
Description: First edition. | New York, NY : Grand Central Life & Style, 2018. | Includes index.
Identifiers: LCCN 2018021723 | ISBN 9781455539987 (paper over board) |
ISBN 9781455539994 (ebook)
Subjects: LCSH: Cooking, American—New York (State)—Brooklyn. | Cooking—New York
(State)—Brooklyn. | Local foods—New York (State)—Brooklyn. | LCGFT: Cookbooks.
Classification: LCC TX715 .A5699 2018 | DDC 641.59747/23—dc23
LC record available at https://lccn.loc.gov/2018021723

ISBNs: 978-1-4555-3998-7 (hardcover), 978-1-4555-3999-4 (ebook)

Printed in the United States of America

WOR

10 9 8 7 6 5 4 3 2 1

RYAN

*I would like to dedicate this book to
my mother, Patricia, who taught me to find what
I love and work hard for it; my grandparents,
Avis and Walter, who reinforced that notion every day;
and Kristen, my beautiful wife, who is the coach,
captain, and cheerleader of "Team Angulo."*

DOUG

*To Laura, my soulmate, best friend,
and compass; Lily, for both her kindness and her salt;
and my parents, for their love and support.*

CONTENTS

INTRODUCTION
KINDNESS & SALT
ix

1
PANTRY
1

2
SALADS & VEGETABLES
37

3
FISH & SHELLFISH
65

4

BIRDS & BEASTS

117

5

BRUNCH

177

WINE
169

CHEESE
173

6

BAKED

219

ACKNOWLEDGMENTS
270

INDEX 272
ABOUT THE AUTHORS 276

7

COCKTAILS

247

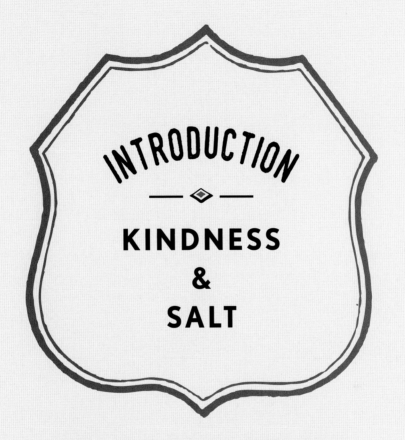

INTRODUCTION

KINDNESS & SALT

WHEN YOU'RE OPENING A RESTAURANT, neighbors peer into your dusty construction site to ask what the place is going to be. We've built two of them from the ground up, and each time we began without a clear answer to that question.

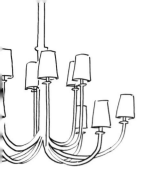

When we met, we were both working at huge, raucous Manhattan restaurants that kept us out until four in the morning. We wanted to come home to Brooklyn, to make the kind of small, friendly restaurant that serves the neighborhood it belongs to.

Brooklyn has the population of a big city (we're bigger than Houston, and gaining on Chicago), but there's no mistaking it for that metropolis on the other side of the bridge. We have a few skyscrapers, but they don't define us. Instead, Brooklyn is a collection of neighborhoods—every one of them a small, proud town.

We searched for a neighborhood that needed a bistro, or our idea of one—a restaurant for all occasions. We envisioned a place where families with kids could share french fries at five o'clock, and dates would begin with Champagne and oysters at eight. A spot you could drop by for an impromptu post-work burger and a beer at the bar with a friend, or reserve a table for six for the "meet the parents" dinner. We would host your blow-out birthday bash—and then be there to nurse you back to life with French toast and bacon the next morning. The room would look great by candlelight or sunlight, and the menu would have something for everyone.

We fixated on a few details, microcosms of the world we wanted to build. For Buttermilk Channel, we envisioned big, fat beer mugs and trestle-leg farm tables. Before we'd even thought of what the signature dishes should be or what to name the place, we knew we wanted to open a restaurant where you would sit with your feet up on that trestle, drinking a beer out of that mug. For French Louie, we imagined marble tabletops, satiny brass, and long banquettes, the kind that make it easy to come around and slide in next to your date. We filled in the rest of the landscape to match these details.

While we wound up with two different restaurants, each with their own style, their spirits are the same—because the two most important things they sell aren't on the menu. Lawyers advertise leases and lawsuits, but they really sell peace of mind. A nail salon really sells foot rubs. A bar sells booze, but you're there for the conversation, a game on TV, a jukebox packed with music you remember. Our menus offer food and drink. But what we really sell is kindness and salt.

Let's start with salt. Our food is pretty straightforward; bistro cuisine is, after all, based in the traditions of home cooking. We're not cutting-edge; you won't have to google the ingredients on your plate. Instead, you'll find uncomplicated food, made carefully with classic technique. The best fried chicken (page 128) is made by marinating a good bird overnight in buttermilk, flouring it an hour in advance to let the crust form, and frying it twice. There may be a new and improved method, something involving meat glue or sous vide, but that's not our style.

Whenever a customer asks us how we get simple food–a roast chicken, a piece of fish, a green bean–to taste so much better than it does at home, the answer is usually salt.

Paying attention to seasoning means cooking carefully, with an eye to bringing out the best in good ingredients. There's the right salt for each dish and the right amount, and you can't just sprinkle it on at the end (see page 32). Salting early and liberally doesn't make things salty; it makes things taste as they should. Our blanching water tastes like the ocean, which means that our pasta tastes like pasta and our green beans taste green. We roast vegetables atop a blanket of salt (see page 59) that seasons them from the outside in. No plate–even at dessert–leaves the kitchen without a final sprinkle.

Salt we buy; kindness answers a help-wanted ad and comes in for an interview. With a little time and tasting, we can teach someone about wine and food; with practice, anyone can learn how to make a killer Negroni or grill a steak. But we can't turn someone into the type of person who will run to the bodega for Sweet'N Low during a busy service because it's what your dad likes in his coffee.

Our staff is a diverse bunch, but there's one fine quality that they all share: they love to take care of people, at our restaurants and at home. If you showed up at their front door, they'd have you on the couch in a minute flat with a drink in your hand, their slippers on your feet, and their cat on your lap. They can't help it, fake it, or turn it off: it's who they are.

Salt isn't listed on our menus, and you won't find kindness called for in our recipes, but we think they're the ingredients that make a good meal great. We hope that you'll season your meals liberally with both–and that you'll have as much fun feeding your family, friends, and neighbors as we do.

Recipes

FOR

SAUCES PICKLES STOCKS JUS PURÉES

CONSERVES CONDIMENTS

21
FOUNDATIONAL
RECIPES

PANTRY

—— ◆ ——

OUR PANTRY, like yours, can be broken into two categories. There are the items that get used all the time, and there's the culinary flotsam that takes up precious space in our crammed kitchens. This chapter is concerned with the first category. These recipes are the building blocks that form the foundation of our everyday cooking—the ingredients we put on and in everything.

AIOLI 4

ANCHO CHILE PURÉE 5

BORDELAISE SAUCE 6

HOLLANDAISE SAUCE 8

BÉARNAISE SAUCE 9

PARSLEY PISTOU 10

I-A SAUCE 12

BUTTERMILK RICOTTA 14

OVEN-DRIED TOMATOES 16

CHICKEN STOCK 17

CARAMELIZED CHICKEN JUS 18

| WHEY 15 | JAM VARIATIONS 25 | SALT 32 |

THE CARE AND FEEDING OF YOUR FRIENDS AND NEIGHBORS
34

PANTRY STAPLES
21

DUCK JUS 19

APPLE BUTTER 20

BLACK PEPPER FIG CONSERVE 22

BLACK OLIVE SALT 23

HUCKLEBERRY JAM 24

BREAD & BUTTER **PICKLES** 26

JARDINIÈRE **PICKLES** 28

DILL PICKLES 29

FRIED CAPERS 30

PICKLED **MUSTARD SEEDS** 31

AIOLI

Makes about 2 cups

2
LARGE EGG YOLKS

1 tablespoon
DIJON MUSTARD

1 tablespoon
DISTILLED
WHITE VINEGAR

1 tablespoon
CHAMPAGNE
VINEGAR

1 clove
GARLIC,
smashed

¼ teaspoon
FINE SEA SALT

1¾ cups
CANOLA OIL

¼ cup
EXTRA-VIRGIN
OLIVE OIL

Aioli is the magical secret ingredient in a number of recipes in this book, lending its tangy richness to everything from baked goods and coleslaw to the best grilled cheese you'll ever eat (page 202). It's also an essential condiment for burgers and french fries.

Combine the egg yolks, mustard, vinegars, garlic, and salt in the bowl of a food processor. Process until the garlic is fully puréed and all ingredients are completely combined. With the motor running, slowly drizzle in the oils and continue to process for another 15 seconds, or until the aioli is completely emulsified. Store in an airtight container, refrigerated, for up to a week.

ANCHO CHILE
PURÉE

Makes about 2 cups

Anchos are dried poblano chiles with a mild, smoky heat. This purée puts the BBQ in our BBQ Oysters (page 76) and Slow-Roasted Pork Spare Ribs (page 143), and enriches our variation on a Portuguese pork and clam stew (page 112).

Split the chiles in half and scrape away the stems and seeds. Pour ¼ inch of oil into a medium sauté pan and gently fry the chiles over medium heat, turning once, until they become blistered, about 1 minute on each side. Transfer the chiles to a plate lined with paper towels to drain. Soak the cooked chiles in a small bowl of warm water for about 20 minutes.

Transfer the chiles to a blender, reserving the soaking liquid. Purée, drizzling in just enough of the soaking liquid to allow the mixture to come together into a thick, smooth paste. Store in an airtight container, refrigerated, for up to a week.

**10
ANCHO CHILES
CANOLA OIL,**
for frying

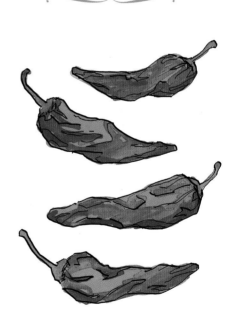

BORDELAISE SAUCE

◈

10 pounds
BEEF BONES,
cut into 2-inch pieces
(ask your butcher)

1 (750 ml) bottle
RED WINE

2 tablespoons
CANOLA OIL

6
SHALLOTS,
chopped

2
LARGE ONIONS,
chopped

6 cloves
GARLIC,
smashed

2
CARROTS,
chopped

1 cup
RUBY PORT

6 quarts
CHICKEN STOCK
(page 17)

1
BAY LEAF

6 sprigs
THYME

1½ teaspoons
**WHOLE BLACK
PEPPERCORNS**

1
**SALT-PACKED WHOLE
ANCHOVY,**
rinsed and boned, *OR*
**2 OIL-PACKED
ANCHOVY FILLETS**

1 strip
ORANGE PEEL
(about 1 inch by 3 inches)

◈

This jazzed-up bordelaise uses chicken stock, which has a nicer flavor than veal or beef. Don't be afraid of the anchovy—its fishiness will disappear, leaving a little umami behind. This sauce can also be the foundation for a rich stew, like our Boeuf Bourguignon "à la Minute" (page 150).

Preheat your oven to 400°F. Spread out the bones in a roasting pan and roast for about 30 minutes, until the bones have become thoroughly browned. Move the roasting pan to the stovetop and set aside the bones. Over low heat, deglaze the pan with the red wine, scraping up all the browned bits from the bottom with a wooden spoon. Set aside.

Heat the canola oil in a stockpot over medium heat and sauté the shallots, onions, garlic, and carrots until they're caramelized. Add the roasted bones to the pot, along with the port and the liquid from the roasting pan. Bring everything to a simmer over medium heat and reduce the liquid until the stockpot is almost completely dry, about 30 minutes. Pour in the chicken stock and add the bay leaf, thyme, peppercorns, anchovy, and orange peel. Bring to a boil, then lower to a gentle simmer. Reduce the liquid by half (this will take about 3 hours), occasionally skimming any fat and impurities that rise to the surface.

Remove the pot from the heat and strain the liquid into a large saucepan, first through a wide-hole strainer or colander and then through a fine-mesh sieve. Bring the liquid to a simmer over low heat and reduce again, skimming frequently, until it's thick enough to coat the back of a spoon, about an hour. Use immediately or cool and store in an airtight container in the refrigerator for up to a week, or in the freezer for up to a month.

HOLLANDAISE SAUCE

Makes about 2½ cups

16 tablespoons (2 sticks)
UNSALTED BUTTER,
melted

5
LARGE EGG YOLKS

JUICE OF ½ LEMON

10 dashes
TABASCO SAUCE

FINE SEA SALT

The usual procedure of whisking egg yolks over a double boiler to make hollandaise is a great way to end up with scrambled eggs and a sore arm. Our recipe uses a blender to do the hard work, and lets the hot butter cook the eggs while it emulsifies with them. The finished sauce will be stable enough to hold for quite a while without breaking.

In a small saucepan, bring the butter just to a boil over high heat; immediately remove the pan from the heat. Combine the egg yolks, lemon juice, and Tabasco in a blender (see note) and process on high speed until the yolks have doubled in size and are pale yellow. At this point the butter should have cooled slightly, but it will still be hot enough to cook the yolks (about 165°F, if you're using a thermometer).

With the blender running, slowly drizzle the butter into the egg yolk mixture. When the butter has been completely incorporated, the sauce should have the consistency of mayonnaise. If it gets too thick, thin it out with a few drops of warm water. Season with salt to taste and use immediately, or hold in a warm water bath for up to an hour.

Note: *An immersion blender also works well for this recipe, but you'll need to use a container that's large enough to protect you from splatters.*

Hollandaise is a "mother" sauce from which a number of other buttery sauces are derived. Its most famous offspring is béarnaise, which exchanges the lemon juice and Tabasco for a reduction of vinegar, tarragon, and shallots. Provided that you like tarragon, this is all good news. Béarnaise is excellent on seafood, steaks, and probably your shoe.

To make the reduction, combine the vinegar, tarragon, and shallots in a small saucepan. Bring to a boil over high heat and reduce by half, about 10 minutes. Strain the reduction through a fine-mesh sieve and reserve (see note).

In a small saucepan, bring the butter just to a boil over high heat; immediately remove the pan from the heat. Combine the egg yolks and 2 tablespoons of the reserved reduction in a blender and process on high speed until the yolks have doubled in size and are pale yellow. At this point the butter should have cooled slightly, but it will still be hot enough to cook the yolks (about 165°F, if you're using a thermometer).

With the blender running, slowly drizzle the butter into the egg yolk mixture. When the butter has been completely incorporated, the sauce should have the consistency of mayonnaise. Adjust the consistency and flavor with a bit more of the reduction, if needed. Season with salt to taste and use immediately, or hold in a warm water bath for up to an hour.

Note: *This recipe yields enough reduction for several batches of béarnaise. The reduction will keep indefinitely in an airtight container in the refrigerator.*

BÉARNAISE
SAUCE

1 cup
WHITE WINE VINEGAR

6 sprigs
TARRAGON

2
SMALL SHALLOTS,
chopped

16 tablespoons (2 sticks)
UNSALTED BUTTER,
melted

5
LARGE EGG YOLKS

FINE SEA SALT

9

PARSLEY
PISTOU

PANTRY

Makes about 2 cups

**2 bunches
FRESH FLAT-LEAF
PARSLEY**
(enough to yield 1 packed cup
of leaves)

**1
SALT-PACKED WHOLE
ANCHOVY,**
rinsed and boned, *OR*
**2 OIL-PACKED ANCHOVY
FILLETS**

**1 large clove
GARLIC,**
smashed

**1 cup
EXTRA-VIRGIN
OLIVE OIL**

At French Louie we call this pistou, the French term for what Italians call pesto. At Buttermilk Channel, where we try to stick to English on our menu, we've struggled to figure out an appropriate name—green sauce? (Sometimes the French just sounds yummier.) The waiters don't always know what to call it, but they know it's the green stuff that tops many of our steaks and grilled fish.

Wash and dry the parsley. Pick the leaves off the thicker stems; keep the tender stems right next to the leaves intact. You should have 1 packed cup.

Combine the parsley, anchovy, and garlic in the bowl of a food processor. Pour in half of the olive oil and process until finely chopped and bright green. Add the rest of the olive oil and process until completely combined, about 2 minutes. Use the pistou immediately or store in an airtight container in the refrigerator for up to a week.

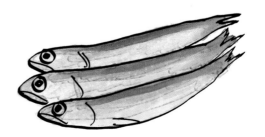

A-1 SAUCE

1 tablespoon
SUGAR

½ cup
WATER

2 cups
DISTILLED WHITE VINEGAR

¾ cup
MOLASSES

1½ tablespoons
TAMARIND PASTE

1 clove
GARLIC,
smashed

1
SMALL ONION,
finely chopped

1
SALT-PACKED WHOLE ANCHOVY,
rinsed and boned, *OR*
2 OIL-PACKED ANCHOVY FILLETS

¾ cup
BLACK RAISINS

2 teaspoons
FINE SEA SALT

½
CINNAMON STICK

1 tablespoon
MUSTARD SEEDS

2 teaspoons
WHOLE BLACK PEPPERCORNS

2 teaspoons
WHOLE CLOVES

2
CARDAMOM PODS,
crushed

1
DRIED CHIPOTLE CHILE

Our house steak sauce is named for Ian Alvarez, our first chef de cuisine, who spent countless vinegary hours tinkering with the ingredients found in Worcestershire and A.1. to create this recipe. It was a pungent process, as you'll discover when you cook a batch for yourself. (Just remember to open a window.) This recipe takes some planning, as the cooked sauce needs about a week in the refrigerator for the ingredients to come together.

In a large saucepan, combine the sugar with ¼ cup of the water and stir to combine. Cook over medium heat until the sugar has become a dark caramel. Turn off the heat and carefully pour in the remaining ¼ cup water–pour very slowly to avoid getting burned by any splatter when the water hits the hot caramel.

Add the vinegar, molasses, tamarind, garlic, onion, anchovy, raisins, and salt to the pan and stir to combine. Bring to a boil over medium heat, then reduce to a simmer.

Meanwhile, in a medium sauté pan, toast all the dry spices and the chipotle over medium heat. When the spices become fragrant, add them to the simmering sauce. Continue to simmer for 20 minutes, stirring occasionally. The sauce will look dark brown and chunky. Cool the sauce and refrigerate in an airtight container for at least 1 week to allow all the flavors to come together. When ready to use, purée the sauce in batches using a blender or immersion blender. Store the sauce in an airtight container in the refrigerator for up to 6 months.

BUTTERMILK
RICOTTA

Makes 2 cups

4 cups
WHOLE MILK

2 cups
HEAVY CREAM

2 cups
BUTTERMILK

1 teaspoon
FINE SEA SALT

This homemade ricotta finds a place inside many dishes and recipes in our restaurants, but it can also stand on its own as the main event. When you pull the warm curds from the pot, take a moment to enjoy a dollop on top of a slice of crusty bread.

Combine all the ingredients in a medium, heavy-bottomed saucepan and cover with a lid. Over low heat, slowly warm the pot, removing the lid to stir four or five times to release any curd that forms on the bottom. As the pot heats up, the curd will form on the surface of the liquid. When it comes to a simmer (this may take an hour or longer), remove from the heat. Gently skim the curd from the pan with a slotted spoon or mesh skimmer into a strainer or colander lined with cheesecloth and set over a bowl. Save the remaining liquid (whey) in the pot for other uses (see box, right).

Allow the ricotta to cool in the cheesecloth to room temperature. Store in an airtight container in the refrigerator for up to 5 days.

14

WHEY

*The whey that's a byproduct of this ricotta is tart and
gently sweet. The Internet is loaded with creative uses for whey—
people bake with it, put it in smoothies, and feed it to their plants and
pets. We always have a ton of leftover whey at our restaurants,
and these are the two things we're most likely to do with it.*

Whey Brine

Whey adds flavor and moisture to "white" meats like pork, chicken, or veal.
Add a couple of sprigs of thyme, a few black peppercorns, a bay leaf, and a
thick strip of lemon zest to the whey and bring it to a simmer for a minute to
allow the flavors to come together. Let the whey cool a bit, then cover
and chill it. Submerge the meat in the whey and marinate, covered and
refrigerated, for a couple of hours or overnight. Drain the meat and pat it dry
before seasoning and cooking.

Carrots Cooked in Whey

1 bunch baby carrots

2 sprigs tarragon

2 cups whey

Put the carrots and tarragon in a pot and cover with the whey. Bring to a boil
and then lower to a simmer. Cook until tender, 8 to 10 minutes.

OVEN-DRIED TOMATOES

Makes as much as you like

RIPE ROMA TOMATOES
FINE SEA SALT
EXTRA-VIRGIN OLIVE OIL

These slow-roasted tomatoes have a deep, concentrated flavor but still retain some juiciness. Use them to garnish a bowl of pasta or a hearty sandwich, like our Lamb Club Sandwich (page 154) or as a fresher-tasting alterative in any recipe that calls for tomato paste.

Preheat your oven to 200°F and line a rimmed baking sheet with parchment paper. Slice the tomatoes in half lengthwise and toss them in a bowl with some salt and enough oil to coat them lightly. Lay the tomatoes, cut side up, in a single layer on the lined baking sheet. Roast for 3 hours, or until the tomatoes have shriveled to about half their original size. Cool to room temperature, then use or store in an airtight container in the refrigerator for up to a week.

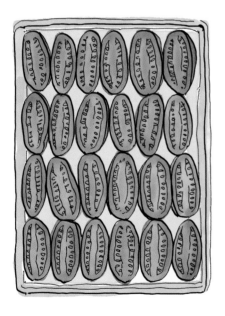

CHICKEN STOCK

Makes about 3 quarts

Whenever you cut up whole chickens at home, save the bones in a bag in your freezer until you have enough to make stock. If you don't have a stash, chicken bones are usually available at any butcher. This stock needs to simmer for a minimum of 2 hours, at which point it will be golden and flavorful. Simmering for as long as 6 hours will produce an even richer, darker stock.

In a large stockpot, cover the bones, vegetables, and herbs with the cold water and bring to a gentle boil over high heat. Lower the heat and simmer for at least 2 hours, skimming and discarding the fat and impurities that rise to the surface. Strain the stock through a fine-mesh sieve and use immediately, or cool and refrigerate or freeze in an airtight container. This stock will keep for up to 5 days in the refrigerator or up to a month in the freezer.

Note: *Starting with cold water helps to slowly extract all the flavor from the bones and vegetables as it comes to a simmer. Never cook with hot water from the tap as it may be contaminated with sediment that builds up in your hot water heater or pipes.*

2 pounds
CHICKEN BONES

1
LARGE CARROT,
chopped

1
LARGE ONION,
chopped

4
CELERY STALKS,
chopped

3 sprigs
THYME

1
BAY LEAF

1 gallon
COLD WATER
(see note)

CARAMELIZED
CHICKEN JUS

Makes about 1 quart

BONES FROM 1 CHICKEN

2 tablespoons
UNSALTED BUTTER

2 cloves
GARLIC,
smashed

2
LARGE ONIONS,
sliced

1 cup
DRY WHITE WINE

2
BAY LEAVES

4 sprigs
THYME

3 quarts
CHICKEN STOCK
(page 17)

This jus takes chicken stock and enriches and reduces it to the point where you could either use it as a sauce or grab a spoon and slurp down a bowl. If you lift out the bones and herbs and leave the onions behind, then top with a garlicky crouton and melted Gruyère, you'll have a delectable French onion soup.

Preheat your oven to 375°F. Spread the bones in a single layer on a rimmed baking sheet or roasting pan and roast until they're golden brown, about 45 minutes.

Meanwhile, melt the butter in a large stockpot over medium-low heat. Add the garlic and onions and cook, stirring frequently, until they are deeply caramelized, about 30 minutes. Add the wine, bay leaves, and thyme to the pot and simmer to reduce by half, about 10 minutes. Add the roasted chicken bones and chicken stock to the pot and bring it to a boil over high heat. Lower the heat to a simmer and reduce the liquid by half again, skimming off the fat and impurities as they rise to the surface; this will take about an hour and a half.

Strain the chicken jus through a fine-mesh sieve and use immediately, or cool and refrigerate or freeze in an airtight container. The jus will keep for up to 5 days in the refrigerator or up to a month in the freezer.

DUCK JUS

Makes about 1 quart

Substituting duck bones for chicken bones produces a jus with a much deeper flavor. This is a sauce for all things duck and also a foundation for other duck sauces.

Preheat your oven to 375°F. Spread the bones in a single layer on a rimmed baking sheet or roasting pan and roast until they're golden brown, about 45 minutes.

Meanwhile, in a large stockpot, heat the oil over medium heat and sauté the onion, garlic, and carrot, stirring frequently, until the vegetables are lightly caramelized, about 10 minutes. Add the roasted duck bones, vinegar, and wine to the pot. Simmer to reduce the liquid by half, about 20 minutes.

Pour in the chicken stock and bring it to a boil over high heat. Lower the heat to a simmer and add the bay leaf, thyme, and star anise. Reduce the liquid by half again, skimming off the fat and impurities that rise to the surface; this will take about an hour and a half.

Strain the duck jus through a fine-mesh sieve and use immediately, or cool and refrigerate or freeze in an airtight container. The jus will keep for up to 5 days in the refrigerator or up to a month in the freezer.

**1 pound
DUCK BONES
(available, maybe with some advance notice, from any butcher that sells duck)**

**2 tablespoons
CANOLA OIL**

**1
LARGE ONION,
chopped**

**2 cloves
GARLIC,
smashed**

**1
LARGE CARROT,
chopped**

**¼ cup
APPLE CIDER VINEGAR**

**2 cups
DRY RED WINE**

**3 quarts
CHICKEN STOCK
(page 17)**

**1
BAY LEAF**

**2 sprigs
THYME**

**2
STAR ANISE,
whole**

APPLE BUTTER

Makes about 1 quart

2½ pounds
APPLES
(about 8 apples, depending on size)

2 cups
WATER

1 cup
APPLE CIDER VINEGAR

2 cups
SUGAR

3 sprigs
ROSEMARY

1 teaspoon
GROUND CINNAMON

1 teaspoon
GROUND CLOVES

1 teaspoon
GROUND GINGER

**GRATED ZEST AND JUICE
OF 1 LEMON**

**GRATED ZEST OF
1 ORANGE**

Any good eating apple works well for this apple butter, and you can tweak the recipe by trying out different varieties. Cortland and Honeycrisp are perfect, and Granny Smiths may be added to the mix for a bit more acidity, or used by themselves if you want an extra-tart apple butter.

Cut the apples into quarters, leaving the peels on and the seeds and stems attached (see note). Put the apple quarters in a medium, heavy-bottomed stockpot and add the water and vinegar. Bring the liquid to a simmer over medium heat and cook until the apples are soft and falling apart, about 20 minutes.

Push the cooked apple mixture through a fine-mesh sieve and then return it to the pot. Add all the remaining ingredients, bring to a boil over medium heat, and then lower to a simmer. As the apple butter thickens it will start to splatter, so keep a lid on (slightly ajar to release the steam), and be careful when stirring. Stir frequently with a rubber spatula to prevent sticking on the bottom of the pot. Cook the apple butter until it has reduced to about 1 quart and takes on a dark caramel color, 45 minutes to an hour. Cool and store in an airtight container in the refrigerator for up to 1 month.

Note: *The apple peels, stems, and seeds contain the natural pectin that will magically thicken this apple butter.*

PANTRY
STAPLES

*The following store-bought ingredients are essential
to our restaurant kitchens and, if you'll be cooking from this book,
to your kitchen as well. We live in small apartments where cabinet
space is scarce, so we won't have you stocking up on giant sacks
of stuff that won't come in handy frequently.*

Bob's Red Mill garbanzo bean flour
(aka chickpea flour)

Amore anchovy paste
(comes in a convenient tube!)

Salt-packed anchovies

Castelvetrano olives

Niçoise olives

Capers

Saltine crackers

Kerrygold butter

Pomì finely chopped tomatoes

Maille Dijon and whole-grain
mustards

Delverde dried pasta

Pastosa fresh pasta
(ships nationwide: Pastosa.com)

Pickled cherry peppers

Extra-virgin olive oil

Banyuls vinegar

BLACK PEPPER FIG
CONSERVE

Makes about 3 cups

2 pints
FRESH BLACK FIGS,
diced

1
SHALLOT,
minced

1 teaspoon
CRACKED BLACK PEPPER

1½ cups
**INEXPENSIVE RUBY
OR TAWNY PORT**
(save the good stuff to
drink after dinner)

½ cup
BALSAMIC VINEGAR

2 teaspoons
CHOPPED FRESH THYME

**FINELY GRATED ZEST OF
1 LARGE ORANGE**

Spread this sweet-savory condiment on your breakfast toast, or use it to accompany game meats or a cheese platter.

Combine the figs, shallot, pepper, port, and vinegar in a medium, heavy-bottomed saucepan. Bring to a gentle boil over medium heat, then reduce the heat and simmer until the liquid has reduced by a third, about 15 minutes. Remove the pan from the heat and stir in the thyme and orange zest. Allow the conserve to cool to room temperature, then serve or store in an airtight container in the refrigerator for up to 2 weeks.

BLACK OLIVE SALT

Makes 2 cups

At French Louie, this salt adds a hit of umami to the traditional French snack of radishes with soft butter (page 54). Once you start finishing dishes with a sprinkle of this stuff, you'll want to put it on everything.

Pat the olives dry between a few sheets of paper towel. In a large saucepan (it needs to hold all the olives in a single layer), heat ½ inch of oil over medium-high heat until it's shimmering hot but not yet smoking. Carefully add the olives to the oil and fry, stirring occasionally, for 15 minutes, or until they are shriveled and completely dry.

Remove the olives from the oil and drain them on a plate lined with dry paper towels. When the olives have cooled to room temperature, mince them until they're about the same size as the grains of coarse sea salt. Mix the chopped olives with the salt and transfer to a dry, airtight container. The olive salt will keep indefinitely in a cool, dry place.

**1 cup
PITTED NIÇOISE OR KALAMATA OLIVES**

CANOLA OIL,
for frying

**1 cup
COARSE SEA SALT**

23

HUCKLEBERRY JAM

Makes about 2 cups

2 cups
FRESH OR FROZEN HUCKLEBERRIES

2 cups
SUGAR

¼ cup
CHAMPAGNE VINEGAR

¼ cup
WHITE VERJUS

½ teaspoon
FINE SEA SALT

Special Equipment

CANDY OR DEEP-FRY THERMOMETER

Making jam is much less intimidating when you take away the gelatin and forgo the canning process. This simple, rustic jam is a perfect accompaniment to a cheese course and a nice alternative to maple syrup on pancakes and French toast. Champagne vinegar (vinegar made from the grape varieties used in Champagne) and verjus (sour grape juice from underripe grapes) are less acidic than most vinegars and are balanced with a bit of sweetness.

Combine all the ingredients in a medium, heavy-bottomed saucepan and stir thoroughly. Bring just to a boil over medium heat and then lower to a simmer. Cook until the temperature reads 220°F on a candy thermometer, about 30 minutes. Allow the jam to cool to room temperature, then refrigerate in an airtight container for up to a month.

JAM VARIATIONS

Blackberry or Blueberry Jam

Substitute fresh or frozen blackberries or blueberries and use 1 cup lime juice in place of the vinegar and verjus.

Strawberry or Raspberry Jam

Substitute fresh or frozen strawberries or raspberries and use 1 cup lemon juice in place of the vinegar and verjus.

BREAD & BUTTER
PICKLES

Makes about 1 quart

**3
LARGE CUCUMBERS**
(any slicing cucumber will work)

**1
SMALL ONION,**
sliced

**½ cup
KOSHER SALT**

**2 cups
CRUSHED ICE**

**1½ cups
DISTILLED WHITE VINEGAR**

**1 cup
SUGAR**

**2 teaspoons
MUSTARD SEEDS**

**2 teaspoons
CELERY SEEDS**

**½ teaspoon
GROUND TURMERIC**

The bread and butter is the classic American pickle: sweet, salty, and sliced into hamburger-ready disks. Because they're sliced before they're pickled, these b&b's are ready to eat much sooner than pickles made from whole cucumbers.

Slice the cucumbers into rounds about ⅛ inch thick. Combine the cucumbers, onion, salt, and ice in a large, nonreactive bowl and mix thoroughly. Cover the bowl and refrigerate overnight.

Drain the cucumber and onion slices in a colander, gently pressing them to remove excess liquid. Transfer the cucumbers and onions to a large jar or other heat-safe container.

Combine the vinegar, sugar, and spices in a small saucepan and bring to a boil over medium heat. Pour the vinegar mixture over the cucumbers and onions and give it all a stir with a spatula or wooden spoon. Allow the pickles to cool, uncovered, to room temperature, then transfer to a container with a tight-fitting lid and refrigerate. These pickles will keep for up to a month in the refrigerator.

JARDINIÈRE PICKLES

Makes about 2 quarts

1 bunch
SMALL CARROTS

4
BABY FENNEL BULBS,
fronds removed

1 cup
LARGE CAULIFLOWER FLORETS

2
HARD GREEN TOMATOES,
cut into wedges

1 cup
TRIMMED STRING BEANS

3 cups
DISTILLED WHITE VINEGAR

2 cups
WATER

½ cup
SUGAR

2 tablespoons
MUSTARD SEEDS

1 tablespoon
FENNEL SEEDS

4
BAY LEAVES

You could use just about any vegetables for these quick pickles. We serve them as a snack at French Louie and use them to garnish our Bloody Marys (page 212) at brunch.

Put all the vegetables in a large, heat-safe container with a tight-fitting lid. Combine the remaining ingredients in a medium saucepan and bring to a boil over high heat. Pour the hot liquid over the vegetables, then cover the container tightly with the lid and leave out to cool to room temperature. Refrigerate overnight before serving. The pickles will keep in an airtight container in the refrigerator for up to a month. They may also be preserved for a longer shelf life using standard canning procedures.

DILL
PICKLES

Makes 32 pickle spears

This classic dill pickle is tart, crunchy, and potent with garlic—maybe not the thing for a first date. Don't use a plastic container for the pickling process; it will smell like garlic for eternity, no matter how much you scrub it.

Pour a ¼-inch layer of salt in a glass baking dish. Place four cucumbers in a single layer in the dish. Pour a heavy seasoning of salt on top. Stack another row of cucumbers on top of the first and salt those the same way (this is not a precise thing; you may have salt left over). Cover the baking dish and transfer the cucumbers to the refrigerator for 24 hours.

Rinse the cucumbers well, then submerge them in ice water for an hour. Cut each cucumber lengthwise into four spears.

Put the garlic, peppercorns, dill, and bay leaves in a glass jar with a tight-fitting lid. If you're using several jars, evenly distribute the ingredients among the jars. Pack the cucumbers tightly into the jars. Pour the vinegar over the cucumbers, making sure they're completely submerged, then cover and transfer them to the refrigerator. After 5 days the pickles will be ready to eat. They will keep for up to 2 months in the refrigerator and may also be preserved for a longer shelf life using standard canning procedures.

6 cups
KOSHER SALT

8
KIRBY CUCUMBERS,
washed and dried

6 cloves
GARLIC,
smashed

2 teaspoons
WHOLE BLACK PEPPERCORNS

½ cup
CHOPPED FRESH DILL

6
BAY LEAVES

4 cups
DISTILLED WHITE VINEGAR

FRIED CAPERS

Makes about 1 cup

1 (6-ounce) jar
CAPERS
(often labeled "nonpareil")

CANOLA OIL,
for frying

These crunchy little guys make a snappy garnish for salads of heartier lettuces, like romaine, or for a chilled soup (page 62). You may even want to consider sneaking them into the multiplex—a handful in a bucket of popcorn makes for a particularly addictive movie snack.

Drain the capers and discard the brine. Heat about 1½ inches of oil in a small saucepan over medium-high heat. Test the oil with one caper; when it begins to sizzle quickly, the oil is ready. Carefully pour all the capers into the oil. Fry, stirring frequently, until the bubbles subside, 3 to 5 minutes. Drain the capers through a fine-mesh sieve and transfer to paper towels to cool. Fried capers will remain crispy for a few days, stored at room temperature in a covered container lined with paper towels.

PICKLED MUSTARD SEEDS

Makes about 2 cups

These seeds pop like caviar between your teeth, adding texture and pungent spice to salads (page 48) and our Steak Tartare (page 125).

Combine the mustard seeds and vinegar in a small saucepan and bring just to a boil over high heat. Remove the pot from the heat and set aside to cool to room temperature. The mustard seeds are now ready to use. They will keep in an airtight container in the refrigerator indefinitely.

1 cup
MUSTARD SEEDS

2 cups
DISTILLED WHITE VINEGAR

AS THE TITLE OF THIS BOOK would suggest, we take our salt seriously. Whether you're grilling fish or baking a cake, it's important to consider how to salt correctly, and which salt you should deploy.

Measuring and substituting: People don't generally make dinner with a scale, so most recipes are measured by volume. In general, measuring salt by volume works fine, provided that you and the recipe's creator are using the same kind. For the same reason that more finely ground coffee makes a stronger cup, substituting a teaspoon of table salt or fine sea salt for a teaspoon of kosher salt will result in a saltier biscuit or bowl of soup.

Even within defined categories like sea salt or kosher, salts often vary widely from brand to brand. If you're accustomed to Diamond kosher salt and you switch to Morton, you'll need to cut back by almost half–it has smaller, denser crystals, which give you more salt in each teaspoon.

Whether or not a measurement is specified, salting "to taste" is always best. No two potatoes or chickens are the same, so the most effective tool for measuring your seasoning is usually your fingers. If you use the same brand consistently, you'll get a feel for how much saltiness comes in each pinch.

When to hold back: When salty ingredients like anchovies, capers, or cheese are due to be added at a later stage, you need to plan accordingly. Salting to taste later will lead to a better result. This also holds true when you're cooking down a liquid to reduce and concentrate–you should salt minimally at first and adjust to taste when the simmering is done.

Kinds of salt: There are four kinds of salt in our kitchens, and a time and place for each. The differences between them aren't in the flavor–they all taste like salt–but in the shapes and textures of their crystals, which affect how consistently they can be measured and whether they will disappear into the food or be a palpable component of a finished dish.

La Baleine Fine Sea Salt: Perfect for seasoning, baking, and general cooking, this is our go-to–unless otherwise specified, all our recipes are made with fine sea salt. It has approximately the same size crystal as table salt but without the weird additives. If you're accustomed to sprinkling with kosher salt, be careful not to use too much.

La Baleine Coarse Sea Salt: These grains are about four times the size of kosher salt, ideal for salt-packing your own anchovies or salt-crusting a whole fish but not practical for general seasoning. It's also a lovely finishing salt for times when you want to add a crunchy, salty pop to a dish.

Morton Kosher Salt: Kosher salt is inexpensive and comes in a big box that's easy to pour from. We use it for salt-baking vegetables and seasoning cooking water. If you use Diamond brand, which is much less dense, you'll need to add significantly more to achieve the same level of seasoning.

Maldon Sea Salt: This salt is only for finishing. You could use it to season your pasta water, but you'd just be pouring money down the drain. Its defining feature is a pyramid-shaped flake that dissolves on your tongue like snow. It's pricey, but you need only a bit, and pretty much everything you cook can benefit from a pinch.

THE
CARE AND FEEDING

OF YOUR FRIENDS AND NEIGHBORS

Buttermilk Channel and French Louie are nestled in two of Brooklyn's many tree-lined brownstone neighborhoods–Carroll Gardens and Boerum Hill, respectively. We opened our doors to these neighborhoods, and soon found that hospitality can go both ways.

It's a real privilege to be invited into people's lives, to watch as the small moments build up to the big ones. We're well stocked with both Champagne flutes and high chairs, and we see how one thing can lead to the other. The Tinder date, the tenth date, the marriage proposal, the rehearsal dinner, the anniversary, the night they don't order wine and won't say why, the newborn strapped to a chest who becomes the baby in the high chair who becomes the kid who tries oysters for the first time. It's the kids who really make you feel the time go by. They grow up fast, while we get older slowly.

Over the years, kindness and salt have blurred the lines between friends, neighbors, staff, and customers. Our restaurants aren't just a spot to get a bite; they serve as the informal post office, a place to leave your spare key, and an emergency source of chicken stock. We dog-sit, lend one another cars, books, power tools, and formal wear. On the Fourth of July, the neighbor with the best roof throws a party, and the rest of us bring the beer and the Frito pie. On New Year's Eve, we pack the restaurant with a thousand black and silver balloons, and after the last fancy dinner is served, the neighborhood pours in for a toast and a kiss. More than once, we've left the diehard dancers with the keys.

The beautiful plates, glasses, and platters in the photos in this book were lent to us by our neighbor Vito, who lives above his antique shop on Atlantic Avenue. An army of our friends and neighbors tested these recipes to make sure they'd taste the same on your plates as they do on ours. They know these dishes better than anyone, after all.

Some of our neighbors have moved; they visit us from other parts of Brooklyn or from places farther away. It's our favorite thing when they come to us straight from the airport. We're here to welcome them home, to reminisce and console. (Yeah. Portland. It must have seemed like a good idea at the time.)

Our restaurants serve countless people, most of whom we haven't yet met. Every day, with kindness and salt, we coax a few more of them into our family.

Recipes
FOR

SALADS GREENS SOUPS
RADISHES SIDES

2

13 FOUNDATIONAL RECIPES

SALADS AND VEGETABLES

BROOKLYN'S FARMERS' MARKETS are a wonderland of gorgeous fruits and veggies—for about half the year.

If we want a salad during the other six months—and we do—we must rely on heartier vegetables and greens that can be stored, preserved, or brought in from warmer climates without losing their finer qualities in the process. Kale ticks those boxes, but given the current craze, how can we be certain there will be any left by the time this book hits the shelves? If you do happen to track down a bunch, massage it vigorously with a clove of garlic, lemon juice, and olive oil and top with freshly grated Parmesan and cracked black pepper. That's a nice salad.

During the happy half of the year when things do grow in our part of the world, much of our produce comes from Snug Harbor Heritage Farm in Staten Island, just a twenty-minute drive away. There, in the large garden that once fed a retirement home for aging sailors, farmer Jon Wilson grows the lettuces, vegetables, herbs, and flowers he delivers to us the day they're picked. The reward we offer the waiters for helping unload crates from Jon's double-parked truck is a few tender lettuce leaves, still warm from the morning sun, or a zebra-striped tomato you can eat like an apple with the juice running down your chin. It's a pretty good deal.

A finished dish takes a bit more preparation, but the guiding principle is non-intervention. When you get the good stuff, get out of the way and let it shine.

GREEN GODDESS SALAD 42

SNUG HARBOR GREENS
WITH TORN HERBS & BANYULS VINAIGRETTE 46

ICEBERG WEDGE
WITH CITRUS FRENCH DRESSING,
TARRAGON & PICKLED MUSTARD SEEDS 48

SUMMER SUGAR SNAP
PEA SALAD 50

ESCAROLE, RADICCHIO,
FENNEL & GRAPE SALAD 51

LEAFY GREENS
WITH TOASTED BREAD CRUMBS &
ANCHOVY VINAIGRETTE 52

RADISHES
WITH BUTTER & BLACK OLIVE SALT 54

STRING BEANS
WITH SAUCE GRIBICHE 55

IN PRAISE OF THE
SALAD SPINNER:
HOW TO CLEAN LETTUCE
44

TOASTING
NUTS
49

LENTIL & WALNUT PÂTÉ 56

CAULIFLOWER & LEEK SOUP
WITH DILL, SCALLION & CARAWAY CRÈME FRAÎCHE 57

SALT-ROASTED BEET HUMMUS 58

CHILLED HEIRLOOM TOMATO SOUP
WITH TORN BREAD CROUTONS 60

CHILLED WHITE ASPARAGUS SOUP
WITH TOASTED ALMONDS 62

GREEN GODDESS SALAD

For the Dressing

1 cup
CRÈME FRAÎCHE

¾ cup
AIOLI (page 4)
OR MAYONNAISE

¾ cup
LIME JUICE
(6 to 8 limes)

1
SALT-PACKED WHOLE ANCHOVY,
rinsed, boned, and minced, *OR*
2 OIL-PACKED ANCHOVY FILLETS,
minced

½ cup
CHOPPED SCALLION

½ cup
FRESH FLAT-LEAF PARSLEY,
chopped

½ cup
FRESH TARRAGON,
chopped

For the Salad

6 strips
BACON

6 heads
LITTLE GEM OR BABY ROMAINE LETTUCE,
washed and dried

2 heads
ENDIVE

FINE SEA SALT

½ cup
CRUMBLED BLUE CHEESE

2
AVOCADOS,
pitted, peeled, and diced

½ cup
SLICED SCALLIONS

This dish takes us back to the era of grand hotel restaurants, when dining rooms had orchestras and floor shows, and chefs in tall toques gave their salad dressings dreamy, romantic names. Green Goddess is an American classic with French roots (aioli, tarragon). It's definitely on the rich end of the spectrum, but it's packed with bright, fresh flavors.

To make the dressing, whisk together the crème fraîche, aioli, lime juice, and anchovy until all ingredients are completely combined. Stir in the scallion and herbs and set aside.

To make the salad, cook the bacon in a sauté pan over medium heat until crispy, then drain on a paper towel. Crumble the bacon and set aside.

Separate the lettuce and endive into leaves and put them in a large bowl. Drizzle about ½ cup of the dressing over the lettuce and endive and toss gently with clean hands. The leaves should be lightly coated. Taste for seasoning and add a bit of salt, if needed. (The bacon and blue cheese will provide most of the salt for this dish, so salt sparingly.)

To serve, arrange a single layer of the dressed lettuces on each plate. Top with some of the bacon, blue cheese, and avocado. Repeat with a second layer. Finish each plate with a generous scattering of sliced scallions.

Any leftover dressing will keep in an airtight container in the refrigerator for up to 5 days.

+ THE GODDESS +

IN PRAISE OF THE SALAD SPINNER: HOW TO CLEAN LETTUCE

*With the exception of iceberg lettuce, which is grown
in Styrofoam or something, salad greens come from dirty places and
should be washed. Just as important as getting the dirt out
of those leaves is drying them completely. Wet lettuce dilutes a
vinaigrette and is one of the leading causes of lame
salads. Unless you want to pat each leaf dry by hand, which is okay
for a small salad, a good salad spinner is essential. Good
means that it's large enough to hold a useful quantity of whole leaves
and that it can spin fast enough to get them dry. The OXO spinner
does a great job and folds up to fit in your smallest cabinet.*

Cleaning Lettuce

Fill a generously sized bowl or pot with cold water and add your salad greens. Use your fingers to get all the leaves separated and agitate them a bit in the water. Let the greens sit for a moment to allow the dirt to settle on the bottom of the bowl.

Lift the greens out of the water with your hands. Dump out your rinse water and run a finger along the bottom of your vessel. If there's any dirt in there, rinse it out, then give the greens another bath or two until the water runs clean.

Dry the greens in your salad spinner in small batches so the leaves have room to move around and get dry on all sides. Give them one good strong spin, then drain the spinner and toss the leaves around. Repeat until the greens are completely dry.

Store lettuces in a bag or bowl with a slightly damp paper towel or dish towel over the top.

SNUG HARBOR GREENS

with Torn Herbs
& Banyuls Vinaigrette

For the Vinaigrette

½ cup
BANYULS VINEGAR
or other aged red wine vinegar

¼ cup
DIJON MUSTARD

1 small
SHALLOT,
finely chopped

1 teaspoon
FRESH THYME LEAVES

½ teaspoon
FINE SEA SALT

1 cup
EXTRA-VIRGIN
OLIVE OIL

For the Salad

8 ounces freshly picked
MIXED LETTUCES,
gently washed and dried

1 cup
MIXED FRESH HERB
LEAVES
(such as flat-leaf parsley,
lovage, chive, basil, tarragon,
and/or dill; see note)

FINE SEA SALT

BLACK PEPPER

The name of this salad comes from the farm in Staten Island where we get our lettuces, spring through fall. Super-fresh lettuces are delicate in flavor and texture and should be handled gently, dressed lightly, and eaten immediately. Banyuls vinegar is a barrel-aged red wine vinegar with mild acidity. It's one of your pricier vinegars—those pretty lettuces deserve the best.

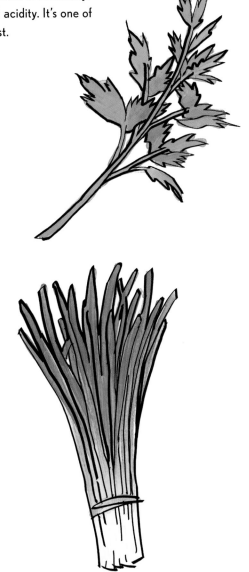

To make the vinaigrette, nestle a mixing bowl in a kitchen towel on your countertop to hold it steady. In it, combine the vinegar, mustard, shallot, thyme, and salt and whisk to combine. Slowly drizzle in the olive oil while whisking with the other hand, until the vinaigrette is completely emulsified.

Combine the lettuces in a large bowl. Tear the herb leaves into large, rough pieces and add them to the lettuces. Gently toss the salad with clean hands to combine.

Dress the salad with the vinaigrette to taste, tossing gently with your hands. Adjust the seasoning with salt, if needed, and finish with a few grinds of pepper.

Any extra vinaigrette will keep in an airtight container in the refrigerator for up to a month.

Note: *The amount of herbs you should use in this salad is a matter of taste. We like to throw in a generous handful so you get herbs in each bite.*

ICEBERG WEDGE

WITH CITRUS FRENCH DRESSING, TARRAGON
& PICKLED MUSTARD SEEDS

Serves 4

For the Dressing

1 cup
OVEN-DRIED TOMATOES
(page 16)

¼ cup
ORANGE JUICE

2 tablespoons
RED WINE VINEGAR

2 tablespoons
DIJON MUSTARD

1 teaspoon
FINE SEA SALT

1½ cups
CANOLA OIL

For the Salad

1 head
ICEBERG LETTUCE

½ cup
PICKLED MUSTARD SEEDS
(page 31)

¼ cup
FRESH TARRAGON LEAVES

Pro tip: when you get to the bottom of this salad, fill your empty bowl with french fries and mop up the dregs. There ought to be a steak frites on the table, so the fries will be close at hand.

To make the dressing, combine the tomatoes, orange juice, vinegar, mustard, and salt in a blender and process until smooth. With the blender running, drizzle in the oil until fully emulsified.

Remove any wilted outer leaves from the lettuce. Cut the head into four even wedges and gently remove the core from each.

To serve, make a small pool of the dressing on each plate. Place a wedge of lettuce, large side down, in the center of the pool. Top the lettuce with another liberal pour of dressing. Scatter some pickled mustard seeds and tarragon leaves on each salad. Any extra vinaigrette will keep in an airtight container in the refrigerator for up to a week.

TOASTING NUTS

Toasted nuts are worth the minor effort involved—
they taste nuttier than their untoasted counterparts, and are
crunchier as well. But they do not permit multitasking. You may not
check your email, chop a clove of garlic, or feed the dog.

You are not allowed to.

Why? Because the second you take your
eyes off your toasting nuts, they will become burned nuts—
an expensive and sometimes recipe-ruining mistake.
Consider yourself warned.

To Toast Nuts

Scatter nuts in a single layer in a sauté pan. Toast over medium heat, tossing frequently, until the nuts give off a nice aroma and are lightly browned, about 5 minutes. Transfer immediately to a bowl or plate to cool.

1 pound
SUGAR SNAP PEAS

1
AVOCADO,
pitted, peeled, and diced

1 cup
FRESH CHERRIES,
pitted

1
MEDIUM SHALLOT,
thinly sliced

¼ cup
LIME JUICE
(2 to 3 limes)

3 tablespoons
PISTACHIO OIL

2 tablespoons
EXTRA-VIRGIN OLIVE OIL

½ cup
FRESH BASIL LEAVES

4 ounces
**PEA GREENS OR PEA
SHOOTS,**
washed and dried

FINE SEA SALT

2 tablespoons
**CHOPPED TOASTED
PISTACHIOS**
(see page 49)

CRACKED BLACK PEPPER

SUMMER
SUGAR SNAP PEA
SALAD

Serves 4

Sugar snap peas are best eaten when they're in season and recently picked, either by a farmer at the local market or by you in your garden, if you are fortunate enough to have such a thing. The pods are tender enough to crunch pleasantly when raw, if you take the time to trim them properly.

To trim the snap peas, remove the fibrous "strings" by gently breaking the tip of the pea at each end and pulling them away. In a large bowl, combine the snap peas with the avocado, cherries, and shallot and toss gently with clean hands. Add the lime juice, pistachio oil, and olive oil, gently toss again, and refrigerate for 10 minutes to allow the ingredients to marinate.

Remove the bowl from the refrigerator and add the basil leaves and pea greens; toss to combine. Season with salt to taste. Divide the salad among four plates. Top with the chopped pistachios and a good amount of pepper.

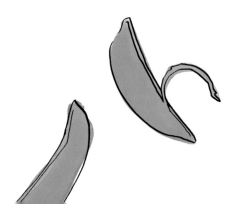

ESCAROLE, RADICCHIO, FENNEL & GRAPE SALAD

Serves 4 to 6

This is a cold-weather salad, something to crunch on when the markets are buried in snow and tomatoes are months away.

Separate the escarole into leaves. Wash in several changes of water and dry thoroughly in a salad spinner. Roughly chop or tear the escarole leaves into 1-inch pieces. Quarter the radicchio head and cut out the core. Cut the radicchio into ribbons about ¼ inch thick. Trim the fennel stalk and fronds away from the bulb. Finely slice the fennel bulb on a mandoline or with a sharp knife and submerge the slices in an ice water bath to retain their crispiness until ready to use. Finely slice the fennel stalk and fronds. Slice the grapes in half.

When ready to serve, drain the sliced fennel. Combine the escarole, radicchio, and fennel bulb and stalk in a large bowl and toss well with clean hands.

Zest the limes and toss the grapes with the zest. Cut the limes in half and squeeze all the juice over the escarole mixture. Toss to coat. Add the olive oil and salt, adjusting both to taste. Divide the dressed salad greens among four or six plates. Top with the halved grapes and season with a few coarse grinds of pepper.

**1 head
ESCAROLE**

**1 head
RADICCHIO**

**1 bulb
FENNEL**

**2 cups
BLACK OR RED SEEDLESS
GRAPES**

**3
LIMES**

**⅓ cup
EXTRA-VIRGIN OLIVE OIL**

FINE SEA SALT

BLACK PEPPER

LEAFY GREENS

with Toasted Bread Crumbs & Anchovy Vinaigrette

For the Vinaigrette

¼ cup
BALSAMIC VINEGAR

1 tablespoon
WORCESTERSHIRE SAUCE

2 tablespoons
WHOLE-GRAIN MUSTARD

1½ teaspoons
DIJON MUSTARD

2 tablespoons
CHOPPED FRESH FLAT-LEAF PARSLEY

1 tablespoon
CHOPPED CAPERS

1
SALT-PACKED WHOLE ANCHOVY,
rinsed, boned, and chopped *OR*
2 OIL-PACKED ANCHOVY FILLETS,
chopped

GRATED ZEST AND JUICE OF 1 LEMON

1 teaspoon
BLACK PEPPER

1 cup
EXTRA-VIRGIN OLIVE OIL

For the Salad

1 pound
MIXED LETTUCES
(such as red leaf, green leaf, red oak, Lolla Rossa, and/or romaine), washed and dried

2 tablespoons
EXTRA-VIRGIN OLIVE OIL

¼ cup
COARSE DRY BREAD CRUMBS

FINE SEA SALT

The vinaigrette for this salad has many of the components of a traditional Caesar dressing, minus the egg yolks and cheese. It won't overwhelm tender lettuces like red leaf or green leaf, but can still hold its own on crunchy romaine. If you're serving kids, don't tell them about the anchovy. They don't always need to know what makes things yummy.

To make the vinaigrette, nestle a mixing bowl in a kitchen towel on your counter to keep it steady. Combine all the vinaigrette ingredients except the olive oil in the bowl and whisk thoroughly to combine. Slowly drizzle in the olive oil while whisking with the other hand to emulsify completely.

To make the salad, first separate the lettuces into whole leaves.

In a medium sauté pan, warm the olive oil over medium heat. Add the bread crumbs to the pan and toast, stirring constantly, until they're golden brown. Remove the pan from the heat and season the bread crumbs lightly with salt while still hot.

In a large bowl, combine the greens and about ¼ cup of the vinaigrette. Toss gently with clean hands and taste. Add more vinaigrette if desired. Season with salt.

To serve, divide the greens among four plates and top with the toasted bread crumbs.

Any extra vinaigrette will keep in an airtight container in the refrigerator for up to a week.

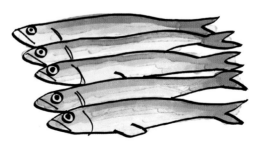

RADISHES

with

BUTTER &
BLACK OLIVE SALT

Serves 4

**2 bunches
RADISHES
(3 to 4 per person)**

**8 tablespoons (1 stick)
HIGH-QUALITY UNSALTED
BUTTER,
at room temperature**

**2 tablespoons
BLACK OLIVE SALT
(page 23)**

Radishes dunked in soft butter, which tames their peppery bite, is a time-honored French snack. Here it gets a slight twist with black olive salt, which adds a briny note.

Remove the tops of the radishes and save for another use (they taste great in salads). Thoroughly wash the radishes and cut if desired. Spread the softened butter onto a plate to a thickness of ¼ inch. Arrange the radishes on top of the butter. Sprinkle the radishes and butter liberally with the black olive salt.

STRING BEANS WITH SAUCE GRIBICHE

Serves 4

Sauce gribiche is a rustic French sauce that's traditionally served alongside fish and charcuterie. It's as good on vegetables as it is on a slice of *pâté grand-mère*; its soft textures are a nice match for a green bean's snappy crunch.

Bring a large saucepan or stockpot of well-salted water to a boil over high heat and prepare a large ice water bath. Blanch the beans until they're cooked through but still firm enough to crunch, then transfer them to the ice water bath to cool.

    Meanwhile, to make the *sauce gribiche*, combine the olive oil, mustards, shallot, cornichons, capers, parsley, eggs, and lemon zest in a large bowl and mix thoroughly. Drain the blanched green beans and add them to the bowl. Mix well and season with salt to taste.

1 pound
STRING BEANS

¼ cup
EXTRA-VIRGIN OLIVE OIL

2 tablespoons
WHOLE-GRAIN MUSTARD

1 tablespoon
DIJON MUSTARD

1
SHALLOT,
finely chopped

10
CORNICHONS,
finely chopped

1 tablespoon
CHOPPED CAPERS

2 tablespoons
**CHOPPED FRESH
FLAT-LEAF PARSLEY**

2
HARD-BOILED EGGS,
chopped

GRATED ZEST OF 1 LEMON

FINE SEA SALT

LENTIL & WALNUT PÂTÉ

Makes about 4 cups

2 tablespoons
CANOLA OIL

1 small
ONION,
roughly chopped

3 cloves
GARLIC,
roughly chopped

½ cup plus 2 tablespoons
TOASTED WALNUTS
(see page 49)

2 cups
BELUGA LENTILS

6 cups
WATER

1
BAY LEAF

¼ cup
WHITE MISO

¼ cup
SOY SAUCE

1 tablespoon
APPLE CIDER VINEGAR

1 tablespoon
FRESH THYME LEAVES

2 tablespoons
EXTRA-VIRGIN OLIVE OIL

The best pâtés are usually made out of animals, sometimes a few of them at once, but this earthy vegan pâté has won the hearts of many committed carnivores. Miso and soy bring the umami to this plant-based party. We serve this pâté with crunchy pickled vegetables and chewy, dark rye bread; you could also use those components to make yourself a hearty sandwich.

In a heavy-bottomed saucepan or Dutch oven, heat the canola oil over medium heat and gently cook the onion and garlic, stirring frequently, until they're translucent, about 8 minutes. Add ½ cup of the toasted walnuts and continue to cook, stirring occasionally, until everything is lightly caramelized. Add the lentils, water, and bay leaf and bring just to a boil. Reduce the heat and simmer, stirring frequently, until all the liquid is absorbed and the lentils are soft, about 30 minutes.

Remove the bay leaf and carefully transfer the cooked lentil mixture to a food processor. Add the miso, soy sauce, vinegar, and thyme and process until smooth. Spread the pâté on a serving dish and allow it to cool. Alternatively, let it cool and then press it into a mold or decorative shape.

To serve, chop the remaining 2 tablespoons of toasted walnuts and sprinkle them over the top of the pâté, then drizzle with the olive oil. This pâté may be served cool or at room temperature and will keep in an airtight container in the refrigerator for up to a week.

CAULIFLOWER & LEEK SOUP

with Dill, Scallion & Caraway Crème Fraîche

Serves 4

This is the kind of soup that warms your bones on a cold winter's day. These Eastern European flavors are calling out for a plate of kielbasa, with spicy mustard and a loaf of pumpernickel. Put on some polka music and break out the vodka!

Melt the butter over medium heat in a large Dutch oven. Add the leek and cauliflower and cook, stirring frequently, until lightly caramelized, about 10 minutes. Add enough water to cover the vegetables halfway, then add the milk and apple cider. Bring to a boil, then lower the heat to a simmer and cook until the cauliflower is soft, about 10 minutes. With a potato masher, gently crush the vegetables in the soup. Season to taste with salt.

In a small bowl, mix the caraway seeds into the crème fraîche. To serve, divide the soup among four bowls. Sprinkle each with some dill and scallion and top with a dollop of the caraway crème fraîche.

2 tablespoons
UNSALTED BUTTER

1 large
LEEK,
white and tender green parts only,
washed and chopped

1 head
CAULIFLOWER,
chopped

1 cup
WHOLE MILK

½ cup
APPLE CIDER OR APPLE JUICE

FINE SEA SALT

1 teaspoon
TOASTED CARAWAY SEEDS
(see page 49)

½ cup
CRÈME FRAÎCHE

2 tablespoons
CHOPPED FRESH DILL

1
SCALLION,
chopped

SALT-ROASTED BEET HUMMUS

The texture of this hummus is similar to the traditional version made with chickpeas, with the earthy sweetness and vibrant red hue that could only come from beets. Roasting the beets on a bed of salt seasons them and also distributes the heat so they cook evenly. We like to serve this hummus on top of a slice of our warm, crispy Chickpea Socca (page 187).

Preheat your oven to 400°F. Spread a ½-inch layer of kosher salt over the bottom of a rimmed baking sheet. Lay the beets on top of the salt. Cover the baking sheet tightly with aluminum foil and place it to roast on the middle rack in the oven. After 1 hour, carefully pull back the foil and check the beets for doneness with a paring knife. If the knife doesn't slide easily through the beets, re-cover the pan and continue to roast, checking every 10 minutes until the beets are fully cooked.

Remove the baking sheet from the oven, uncover, and allow the beets to cool to room temperature. Peel the cooled beets with a paring knife and cut them into large chunks. (The salt may be saved in an airtight container and used for future salt-roasting.)

Transfer the beet chunks to a food processor and add the garlic, tahini, lemon juice, and sea salt. Process until smooth, scraping down the sides of the bowl a few times with a rubber spatula. With the motor running, drizzle in the olive oil and process for about 15 seconds, until it's completely emulsified. Taste and add more salt, if needed.

Serve at room temperature. Any leftover hummus will keep in an airtight container in the refrigerator for up to a week.

**1 pound (approximately)
KOSHER SALT,**
for roasting

**2½ pounds
RED BEETS,**
washed and dried

**6 cloves
GARLIC,**
smashed

**1 cup
TAHINI**

JUICE OF 1½ LEMONS

**1 teaspoon
FINE SEA SALT,**
plus more to taste

**¼ cup
EXTRA-VIRGIN OLIVE OIL**

CHILLED
HEIRLOOM TOMATO SOUP
WITH TORN BREAD CROUTONS

This is a soup to make when all the tomatoes are bursting their skins with ripeness. They're delicious today and will be rotten tomorrow—emergency! It's reminiscent of the smoother, emulsified type of gazpacho, one of countless styles you'll find in Spain. Rather than floating the oil on top, you blend it in completely to give the soup a creamy texture.

In a blender, process the tomatoes, shallots, and vinegar until smooth. With the blender running, drizzle in the canola oil and ¼ cup of the olive oil and blend until emulsified. If your blender can't accommodate all the ingredients at once, blend in two batches, emulsifying half of the oils into each batch. Season to taste with salt and refrigerate to chill completely.

Meanwhile, preheat your oven to 350°F. Remove the crust from the bread and discard (or save to make bread crumbs). Tear the bread into 1-inch pieces and toss in a bowl with the remaining ¼ cup of olive oil and a pinch of salt. Spread out the croutons in a single layer on a rimmed baking sheet and toast until they're golden brown at the edges, about 10 minutes. Allow the croutons to cool completely on the baking sheet.

To serve, divide the soup among six chilled soup bowls and top with the croutons. Any remaining croutons will keep in an airtight container for up to a week.

**4
LARGE HEIRLOOM
TOMATOES,**
roughly chopped

**2
SHALLOTS,**
roughly chopped

**4 teaspoons
BANYULS VINEGAR OR
OTHER AGED RED WINE
VINEGAR**

**½ cup
CANOLA OIL**

**½ cup
EXTRA-VIRGIN OLIVE OIL**

FINE SEA SALT

**½ loaf
UNSLICED COUNTRY BREAD**

CHILLED
WHITE ASPARAGUS SOUP

with Toasted Almonds

For the Soup

**½ cup
EXTRA-VIRGIN
OLIVE OIL**

**2
ONIONS,**
sliced

**6 cloves
GARLIC,**
smashed

**2 pounds
WHITE ASPARAGUS,**
roughly chopped,
woody stems and all

**1 cup
TOASTED ALMONDS**
(see page 49)

**4 cups
WHEY**
(page 15)
OR WATER

FINE SEA SALT

To Garnish

**½ cup
CHOPPED HARD-
BOILED EGGS**

**¼ cup
TOASTED ALMONDS**

**2 tablespoons
FINELY CHOPPED RED
ONION**

**2 tablespoons
CHOPPED FRESH DILL**

**2 tablespoons
FRIED CAPERS**
(page 30)

Eggs and almonds share an affinity for asparagus, and they combine forces in the garnish for this soup. Leftover whey from our Buttermilk Ricotta (page 14) adds a lovely sweet-tangy dimension, but you won't miss it if you make the soup with plain old water.

In a large stockpot, heat the olive oil over medium-low heat. Gently sauté the onions and garlic, stirring frequently, until the vegetables are translucent, about 10 minutes. Add the asparagus, almonds, and whey to the pot and bring just to a boil over high heat. Reduce the heat and simmer for 15 minutes, or until the asparagus is soft.

With an immersion blender, blend the soup until smooth. Season with salt to taste. Chill the pot of soup completely in an ice water bath or the refrigerator, at least 1 hour or overnight.

Divide the soup among eight chilled bowls, scatter all the ingredients for the garnish over the surface, and serve. Any leftover soup will keep in the refrigerator for up to a week.

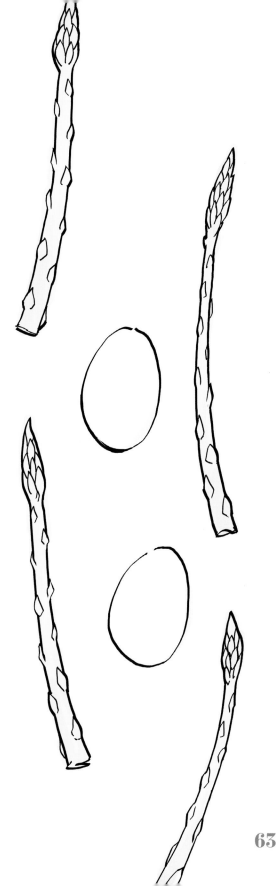

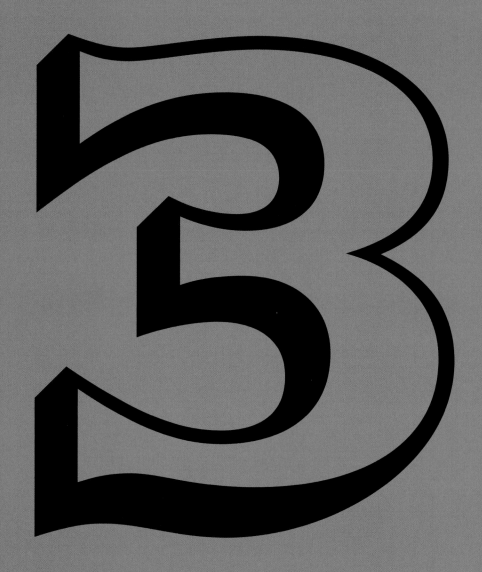

Recipes

FOR

OYSTERS SARDINES MUSSELS

LOBSTER SCALLOPS TROUT BLUEFISH

FISH

AND

SHELLFISH

ONE OF BROOKLYN'S LITTLE-KNOWN SECRETS is that it's a great fishing town. Go down to Sheepshead Bay before seven any morning and you'll find a battalion of charter boats ferrying Brooklynites off to sea in pursuit of striped bass, porgy, bluefish, and the occasional cod. Meanwhile, some of the best oysters in the East snooze in chilly beds along the nearby Long Island Sound, munching on plankton in preparation for their date with a cocktail fork and a lemon wedge.

Because it's so good and so plentiful, we use as much local seafood as we can, and we never forget that it's a natural resource that we have a responsibility to preserve. We save the glamour fish for holidays and fill our menus with sustainable options that are no less delicious.

OYSTERS
73

AT THE FISH MARKET 99

HOW TO
STORE FISH
102

CHILLED EAST BEACH BLONDE OYSTERS

WITH GRAPEFRUIT MIGNONETTE 70

OYSTERS WITH SALTINES 74

BBQ OYSTERS 76

OYSTERS **BIENVILLE** 78

ANCHOVY FRITES 80

SMOKED SARDINES

WITH DULSE BUTTER & RYE FICELLE 82

WARM LOBSTER COCKTAIL 85

MUSSELS **NORMANDE** 88

MUSSELS **PIPÉRADE** 90

NARRAGANSETT STEAMED MUSSELS

WITH CHERRY PEPPERS, BASIL & OLIVES 93

SEARED SCALLOPS

WITH BRUSSELS SPROUTS & CIDER BROWN BUTTER 94

CRISPY SKATE WING

WITH CRAB BISQUE & DIRTY RICE 96

GRILLED BLUEFISH

WITH CRANBERRY BEAN & LINGUIÇA STEW 100

GRILLED WHOLE PORGY

WITH GREEN TOMATO SAUCE VIERGE 104

BENTON'S HAM–WRAPPED TROUT

WITH MUSTARDY MUSTARD GREENS 106

PARSLEY-CRUSTED HAKE

WITH SUMMER BEANS 108

FLOUNDER GRENOBLOISE 110

PORTUGUESE-STYLE **PORK & CLAMS** 112

| TOMATO CONCASSÉ 105 | AT THE DOOR 114 |

CHILLED
EAST BEACH BLONDE OYSTERS

WITH GRAPEFRUIT MIGNONETTE

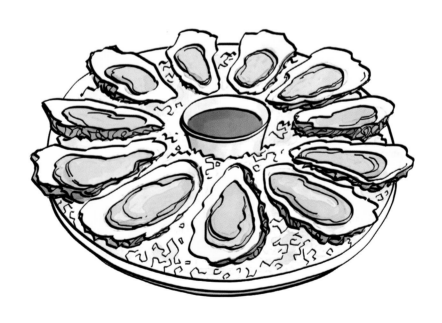

East Beach Blondes, from Ninigret Pond in Rhode Island, are plump, sweet, and as briny as an ocean breeze. Other East Coast oysters will do the trick, but for us, this one is the ideal.

With a sharp paring knife, cut the peel and white pith off the top and bottom of the grapefruit. Sit the grapefruit on one of its cut ends and, using a sawing motion along its curvature, trim all the remaining peel and pith from the fruit. Hold the peeled grapefruit in the palm of your hand and gently cut away the segments from between the white membranes (see note).

    Put the citrus segments in a small bowl and squeeze the rest of the juice out of the fruit into the bowl. Stir in the shallot, pepper, and vinegar. Chill the mignonette until ready to serve.

    With an oyster knife, remove the top shells from the oysters and cut the adductor muscles to release the meat from the shells. Leave the oysters in their bottom shells. Spread a layer of crushed ice on top of a clean kitchen towel in a serving bowl or platter. Nestle the oysters in the ice and put the bowl of mignonette in the center. Serve with oyster forks, if you have them, and top with a splash of mignonette, or just slurp right from the shells.

Note: *French chefs call these citrus segments suprêmes. Isn't that nice?*

**1
RUBY RED GRAPEFRUIT**

**1 tablespoon
finely chopped
SHALLOT**

**2 teaspoons
BLACK PEPPER**

**¼ cup
RED WINE VINEGAR**

**12
EAST BEACH
BLONDES OR OTHER EAST
COAST OYSTERS**

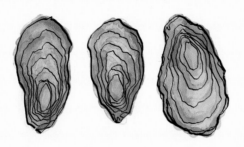

OYSTERS

As luxury items go, oysters are pretty cheap. Once you learn how to open them—and there are countless videos online to show you how—serving them at home is a breeze. Open them just before serving, and sniff each one as you plate it. A bad oyster will smell unambiguously bad; you'll be doing your guests a real favor.

Once opened, oysters can be dressed up or down. A platter of cleanly shucked bivalves on a bed of crushed ice alongside a bottle of Champagne is the perfect opening act for an elegant occasion. A cold beer and a pile of oysters served with saltines, butter, and hot sauce on the side is no less decadent.

OYSTERS
WITH
SALTINES

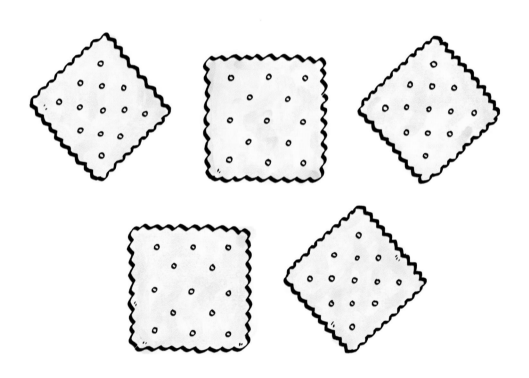

This canapé marries the New Orleans tradition of eating oysters on crackers with the French tradition of putting butter on everything. Butter has a starring role in this show, so it's worth upgrading to one of the widely available European brands like Plugrá or Kerrygold. Better still, try a cultured butter from a local dairy.

With an oyster knife, remove the top shell from the oysters and cut the adductor muscles to release the meat from the shells.

To make a canapé for passing, generously butter the crackers and top each with a shucked oyster and a dash of hot sauce.

If you're going family style, spread a layer of crushed ice on top of a clean kitchen towel in a serving bowl or serving platter. Arrange the opened oysters, still in their bottom shells, on the ice and serve immediately alongside a dish of saltines, the softened butter, and a bottle of hot sauce.

12
OYSTERS
(preferably briny East Coast oysters)

8 tablespoons (1 stick)
HIGH-QUALITY
UNSALTED BUTTER,
at room temperature

12
SALTINE CRACKERS

HOT SAUCE
(try Crystal brand if you want to stay true to this dish's New Orleans roots)

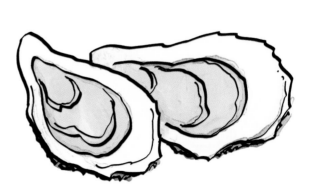

BBQ
OYSTERS

For the BBQ Sauce

**2
SHALLOTS,**
roughly chopped

**2 cloves
GARLIC,**
smashed

**¼ teaspoon
CHOPPED FRESH
GINGER**

**¼ cup
TOMATO PASTE**

**2½ tablespoons
SOY SAUCE**

**2 tablespoons
LEMON JUICE**

**2 tablespoons
APPLE CIDER
VINEGAR**

**2 tablespoons
ANCHO CHILE PURÉE**
(page 5)

**2 tablespoons
DARK BROWN SUGAR**

**¾ teaspoon
CHILE FLAKES**

For the Oysters

**2 strips
BACON**

**12
MEDIUM OYSTERS**

KOSHER SALT

**1
LEMON,**
cut into wedges

**1
SCALLION,**
finely sliced

While this sauce is barbecue-inspired, the oysters themselves are served almost raw. When you remove them from the oven, the oysters should be just warmed through and will have retained their "liquor." This BBQ sauce also makes a great spicy cocktail sauce for chilled shellfish.

To make the BBQ sauce, combine all the ingredients in the bowl of a food processor and pulse until combined but still chunky. Refrigerate until ready to serve.

Preheat your oven to 450°F.

In a small sauté pan, cook the bacon over medium heat until crispy, then drain on a paper towel. Roughly chop the bacon.

With an oyster knife, remove the top shells from the oysters and cut the adductor muscles to release the meat from the shells. Leave the oysters in their bottom shells. Prepare a rimmed baking sheet with 12 little mounds of salt (to keep the oysters in place while cooking). Place an oyster on top of each mound, taking care to avoid spilling any of the oyster liquor. Top each oyster with ¼ teaspoon of the BBQ sauce and a pinch of the bacon bits. Bake for about 2 minutes, until the oysters are just warmed through. Arrange the oysters on a platter around the lemon wedges and garnish with the sliced scallions.

Any leftover BBQ sauce will keep in an airtight container in the refrigerator for up to a week or in the freezer for up to a month.

OYSTERS BIENVILLE

2 tablespoons
UNSALTED BUTTER

½ cup
finely chopped
BUTTON MUSHROOMS

1
SHALLOT,
finely chopped

¼ cup
DRY SHERRY

4 ounces
LUMP CRABMEAT
(or substitute chopped cooked
shrimp for a dish more like
Arnaud's)

FINE SEA SALT

12
MEDIUM OYSTERS

KOSHER SALT

¾ cup
HOLLANDAISE SAUCE
(page 8), kept warm

2 tablespoons
**CHOPPED
FRESH CHIVES**

1
LEMON,
cut into wedges

Oysters Bienville is a New Orleans classic, invented at Arnaud's in the French Quarter in the 1930s. While it's traditionally prepared with shrimp and oysters from the Gulf Coast, we use crabmeat and East Coast oysters—although any oyster would be great with this stuff on it. Six of these and a salad would make a beautiful lunch.

Preheat your oven to 450°F.

In a medium sauté pan, melt the butter over medium heat and sauté the chopped mushrooms and shallot, stirring frequently, until they're lightly caramelized, about 10 minutes. Deglaze the pan with the sherry and reduce the liquid until it's almost dry (*au sec*, as they'd say at Arnaud's). Turn off the heat, mix in the crabmeat, and season with a pinch of sea salt. Allow the mushroom mixture to cool a bit in the pan before using it in the next step.

With an oyster knife, remove the top shells from the oysters and cut the adductor muscles to release the meat from the shells. Leave the oysters in their bottom shells. Prepare a rimmed baking sheet with 12 little mounds of kosher salt (to keep the oysters in place while cooking). Place an oyster on top of each mound, taking care to avoid spilling any of the oyster liquor.

Fold the mushroom mixture (which should still be warm, but not steaming hot) into the hollandaise and top each oyster with a generous dollop. Bake the oysters until they're golden brown, 8 to 10 minutes. Sprinkle with the chives and serve with wedges of lemon.

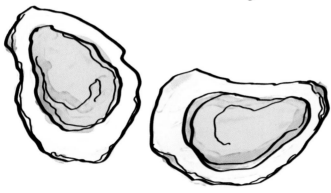

ANCHOVY FRITES

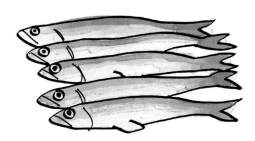

1 pound
FRESH ANCHOVIES

1½ cups
BUTTERMILK

2 cups
ALL-PURPOSE FLOUR

2
LEMONS

CANOLA OIL,
for frying

FINE SEA SALT

½ cup
**FRESH FLAT-LEAF
PARSLEY LEAVES**

AIOLI
(page 4)

Special Equipment

**CANDY OR DEEP-FRY
THERMOMETER**

When our neighbor, the wonderful food historian, cookbook writer, professor, and journalist Dr. Jessica B. Harris comes to dinner at French Louie, she likes to get an order of these anchovies for each person at her table. We can imagine no higher praise. Be warned: they are addictive. The lemons aren't just there to look pretty; the bitter, citrusy wheels are a lovely contrast to these fatty little fish.

Sort through the anchovies and discard any fish that are not firm to the touch. If you don't want to look at their heads as you eat, you can cut them off, but it's not necessary. Pour the buttermilk into a bowl and dump all the anchovies in. Pour the flour into a shallow dish and then use your fingers to dredge each anchovy individually. Set aside on a clean dish for frying. Reserve the buttermilk for the lemons.

Slice the lemons into thin rings and dunk them in the buttermilk, then dredge them in the flour. Set the anchovies and lemons aside for at least 20 minutes before frying. During this time their exteriors will go from floury to sticky, ensuring that the crust will stick to the fish while frying and become crunchy when cooked.

Pour 2 to 3 inches of oil into a large saucepan with a tight-fitting lid. Using a candy thermometer to measure, heat the oil to 350°F over medium heat. Working in batches, fry the anchovies in a single layer, moving them around from time to time with a slotted spoon so they cook evenly. Fry each batch until they're crispy and golden, about 3 minutes. Transfer the anchovies to a plate or tray lined with paper towels to drain, and season with salt immediately. Fry the lemon slices in the oil until they're golden brown, transfer to the paper towels to drain, and season with salt.

Next fry the parsley, but be ready to put a lid on the pan immediately because the oil will splatter when the parsley hits it. Fry for 30 seconds, or until the oil quiets down and the leaves become translucent. Using a slotted spoon, transfer the parsley to the paper towels to drain, and season with salt.

Pile the anchovies, fried lemon slices, and parsley on a plate and serve with a small bowl of aioli for dipping.

SMOKED SARDINES

with Dulse Butter & Rye Ficelle

¼ cup
DRIED DULSE FLAKES

16 tablespoons (2 sticks)
UNSALTED BUTTER,
at room temperature

1 packed cup
DARK BROWN SUGAR

½ cup
FINE SEA SALT

4 cups
**ROOM-TEMPERATURE
WATER**

2 cups
ICE WATER

6
FRESH SARDINES

CANOLA OIL,
for greasing

1 loaf
**RYE FICELLE OR
OTHER RYE BREAD**

Special Equipment

**GAS OR CHARCOAL
GRILL WITH A LID**

WIRE RACK
large enough to hold the
sardines in a single layer

**DISPOSABLE
FOIL PAN**
large enough to hold the wood
chips but slightly smaller than
the wire rack

2 cups
**HICKORY OR
APPLEWOOD CHIPS**

Dulse is a seaweed, found off both the Atlantic and Pacific coasts, that develops an amazing umami flavor when dried. We serve these sardines on slices of an extra-chewy rye ficelle (similar to a baguette, but thinner) from the wonderful Bien Cuit bakery on Smith Street, around the corner from French Louie. If your bakery does not make a rye ficelle, substitute another rye bread.

Put the wood chips in a bowl of water and leave them to soak for at least an hour.

Mix the dulse flakes into the softened butter in a small bowl. Scrape the dulse butter onto a layer of plastic wrap and shape into a tube about 1½ inches in diameter. Seal and refrigerate until the butter is firm.

Meanwhile, to make the brine, combine the sugar, salt, and room-temperature water in a saucepan and stir over medium heat until all the sugar and salt have dissolved. Remove the pan from the heat and pour in the ice water. The brine needs to be cold; if it's still warm after the ice has melted, put it in the refrigerator, uncovered, until fully chilled.

Hold the sardines under a steady stream of running water and gently scrape away the scales with a paring knife, working from tail to head and taking care not to tear the skin. On a cutting board, use the paring knife to cut the fillets from each side of the spine. Gently scrape away any blood from the flesh side of the fish. Cut away the belly bones from the fillets. Leave the tiny pin bones in; they'll dissolve during the cooking process. Submerge the sardine fillets in the chilled brine, and leave them to them cure in the refrigerator for 30 minutes.

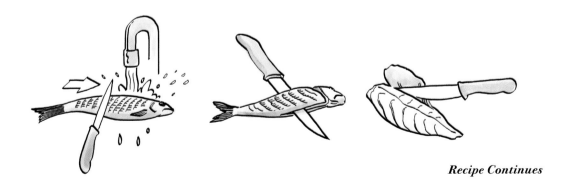

Recipe Continues

Preheat the grill on high heat. Remove the sardines from the brine and arrange them, skin side up, in a single layer on the wire rack. Drain the wood chips completely. Poke about a dozen holes in the bottom of the disposable foil pan with a pen or knife and dump the wet wood chips into the pan. Put the pan on the grill and close the lid. When the chips are smoking, place the rack of sardines over the top of the pan. Close the lid and let the fish cook in the smoke for 2 to 3 minutes, until they are cooked through. Carefully remove the rack from the grill and allow the sardines to cool to room temperature. Lightly oil a plate and lay the sardines on it in a single layer. Cover with plastic wrap and refrigerate until chilled, about 2 hours. Chilled sardines will hold in the refrigerator for 5 days.

To serve, slice the rye bread on a bias about the length of the sardines. Remove the dulse butter from the plastic wrap and cut into ¼-inch-thick rounds. Arrange the chilled smoked sardines on a serving plate, top with rounds of butter, and serve alongside the rye bread slices.

WARM
LOBSTER
COCKTAIL

---

2 (1¼- to 1½-pound)
LIVE LOBSTERS

1 cup
CORNMEAL

1 cup
RICE FLOUR

2 tablespoons
ESPELETTE PEPPER *OR*
1½ teaspoons
CAYENNE PEPPER

2 tablespoons
PAPRIKA

2 tablespoons
FINE SEA SALT

4 tablespoons (½ stick)
UNSALTED BUTTER

4 sprigs
TARRAGON

2
LEMONS,
cut in half

BÉARNAISE SAUCE
(page 9)

Recipe Continues

Makes 4 appetizer-size servings

This is a user-friendly lobster. All the messy work is done in the kitchen, so you can leave your bibs and crackers in the drawer. Espelette is a gentle, slightly smoky pepper from southeast France. It's available online and in stores that sell fancier spices. If you pick up some for this dish, you'll soon find yourself reaching for it all the time.

Bring a large stockpot of water to a boil over high heat and prepare an ice water bath in a second large pot or bowl. Drop the lobsters into the boiling water and cook for 7 minutes, then plunge them immediately into the ice water bath. (If multiplying this recipe, blanch no more than two lobsters at a time.) Allow the lobsters to cool in the ice water bath for about 7 minutes, adding more ice, if needed, to maintain a frigid temperature.

With a firm grip on the lobster bodies, rip off the claws and knuckles. Flip the lobsters on their backs and, using a sharp, sturdy chef's knife, cut them in half lengthwise from head to tail. Tear the knuckles apart from the claws. Hold the claws by their tips and carefully crack them on both sides with the back edge of the chef's knife or lobster crackers, if you have them. Gently pull away the bottom part of the shell from the claw. Using a small pair of sharp scissors, trim open the knuckles lengthwise on both sides, removing the meat as you go.

In a shallow baking dish, mix the cornmeal, rice flour, espelette pepper, paprika, and salt. Place the lobster parts, flesh side down, in the seasoned flour.

In a large, heavy-bottomed sauté pan, melt the butter over medium heat. When the butter becomes foamy, lay the lobster pieces in the pan, floured side down (if you don't have a pan large enough to hold all the lobster, cook in batches). Add the tarragon to the pan and cook for 1 to 2 minutes, until a nice, golden crust has formed on the lobster. Flip the lobster pieces and continue to cook for an additional minute.

Remove the lobster from the pan and divide among four plates. Give each plate a lemon half and a generous bowl of béarnaise sauce for dipping. Garnish with the crispy tarragon sprigs.

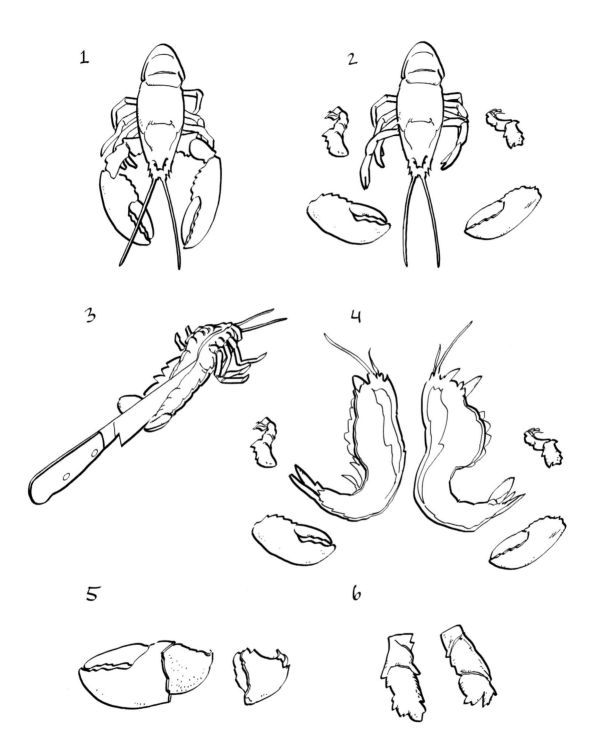

1

2

3

4

5

6

MUSSELS
NORMANDE

2 pounds
MUSSELS

2 tablespoons
UNSALTED BUTTER

2 large
LEEKS,
white and tender green parts
only, washed and sliced

½ cup
SLICED CELERY

1 (12-ounce) bottle
HARD CIDER

4 slices
COUNTRY BREAD
(about ½ inch thick)

½ cup
**CRÈME FRAÎCHE OR
SOUR CREAM**

¼ cup
DIJON MUSTARD

¼ cup
**WHOLE-GRAIN
MUSTARD**

1 teaspoon
FINE SEA SALT

APPLE BUTTER
(page 20)

These are mussels that stick to your ribs, a perfect lunch for a chilly winter day. Normandy is famous for its shellfish, dairy, apples, and cider—all of which play together nicely in this dish. Use a medium-dry hard cider, like Doc's from Warwick, New York, and buy a second bottle to drink.

Put the mussels in a colander and rinse them thoroughly with cold water. Pull the beards to remove them from the shells, and rub away any other debris with your fingers or a brush. Throw away any open mussels that do not immediately close when tapped. Store the mussels in the refrigerator, under a damp towel, until ready to cook.

Melt the butter in a stockpot or Dutch oven over medium heat. Add the leeks and celery and cook, stirring frequently, until translucent, about 5 minutes. Pour in the cider and bring to a boil over high heat. Add the mussels, give them a quick stir, and cover the pot with a lid. Cook the mussels, stirring occasionally, until they open, 5 to 10 minutes, depending on their size.

While the mussels are cooking, toast the country bread in a broiler or toaster oven until golden brown. In a small mixing bowl, stir together the crème fraîche, mustards, and salt. Set aside.

After the mussels open, add the crème fraîche mixture and stir until the mussels are well coated and creamy, then remove the pot from the heat. Divide the mussels among four bowls, discarding any that haven't opened. Give each piece of toast a generous schmear of apple butter and prop one on top of each bowl.

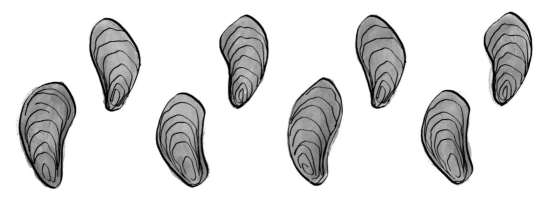

MUSSELS PIPÉRADE

2 pounds
MUSSELS

½ cup
**EXTRA-VIRGIN
OLIVE OIL**

1
ONION,
sliced

2 cloves
GARLIC,
sliced

2
**ROASTED RED
PEPPERS,**
sliced

½ cup
**SLICED
CASTELVETRANO
OR OTHER GREEN
OLIVES**

1
BAY LEAF

¼ cup
RED WINE VINEGAR

¼ cup
DRY WHITE WINE

FINE SEA SALT

2 tablespoons
**CHOPPED FRESH
FLAT-LEAF PARSLEY**

2 tablespoons
**TOASTED BREAD
CRUMBS**

The sauce for these mussels is a variation on a Basque stew traditionally made of sweet peppers, onions, and tomatoes. Our pipérade lost its tomatoes and picked up some green olives on the trip to Brooklyn, but it still contains the three colors of the Basque flag—red, white, and green—that are its patriotic signature. This stew is also the key component of one of our most popular brunch dishes at French Louie, the Pipérade & Merguez Scramble (page 201).

Put the mussels in a colander and rinse them thoroughly with cold water. Pull the beards to remove them from the shells, and rub away any other debris with your fingers or a brush. Throw away any open mussels that do not immediately close when tapped. Store the mussels in the refrigerator, under a damp towel, until ready to cook.

To make the pipérade, heat the olive oil in a stockpot or Dutch oven over medium heat. Add the onion and garlic and cook, stirring frequently, until translucent, about 10 minutes. Add the roasted peppers, olives, bay leaf, and vinegar. Lower the heat and simmer for 5 minutes.

Pour in the white wine and turn the heat up to high. Add the mussels to the pot, give them a good stir, and cover the pot with a lid. Cook the mussels, stirring occasionally, until they open, 5 to 10 minutes, depending on their size. Season with salt to taste. Divide the mussels and broth among four bowls, discarding any that haven't opened. Top with the parsley and toasted bread crumbs and serve immediately.

NARRAGANSETT STEAMED MUSSELS

WITH CHERRY PEPPERS, BASIL & OLIVES

Makes 4 appetizer-size servings

We used to change up the mussels seasonally at Buttermilk Channel, but this dish got so popular that we can't ever take it off the menu. You could use a different beer if Narragansett isn't available, or if you've got some kind of beef with Rhode Island.

Put the mussels in a colander and rinse them thoroughly with cold water. Pull the beards to remove them from the shells, and rub away any other debris with your fingers or a brush. Throw away any open mussels that do not immediately close when tapped. Store the mussels in the refrigerator, under a damp towel, until ready to cook.

Pour the beer into a stockpot or Dutch oven and add the garlic, peppers, and olives. Bring the beer to a boil over high heat, add the mussels and butter, give them a good stir, and cover. Cook the mussels, stirring occasionally, until they open, 5 to 10 minutes, depending on their size. Toss in the basil and salt.

Divide the mussels and broth among four bowls, discarding any that haven't opened. Serve immediately with the crusty Italian bread on the side to mop up the broth.

2 pounds
MUSSELS

1 (24-ounce)
TALLBOY NARRAGANSETT LAGER
(or substitute any pilsner or lager)

4 cloves
GARLIC,
chopped

6
PICKLED RED CHERRY PEPPERS,
finely chopped

½ cup
SLICED GREEN OLIVES

8 tablespoons (1 stick)
UNSALTED BUTTER

¼ cup
TORN FRESH BASIL LEAVES

2 teaspoons
FINE SEA SALT

LOTS OF CRUSTY ITALIAN BREAD

SEARED SCALLOPS

*with Brussels Sprouts
& Cider Brown Butter*

For the Cider Brown Butter

**2 cups
APPLE CIDER**

**6 tablespoons
UNSALTED BUTTER**

For the Brussels Sprouts

**2 tablespoons
UNSALTED BUTTER**

**1 pound
BRUSSELS SPROUTS,
thinly sliced**

**2
APPLES,
peeled, cored, and diced small**

**¼ cup
DRIED CRANBERRIES**

**1 teaspoon
GROUND CINNAMON**

**1 tablespoon
CHOPPED FRESH
FLAT-LEAF PARSLEY**

FINE SEA SALT

For the Scallops

**8
LARGE SEA SCALLOPS**

FINE SEA SALT

**CANOLA OIL,
for sautéing**

**2 tablespoons
CHOPPED TOASTED
WALNUTS**
(see page 49)

When shopping, look for scallops labeled "dry," meaning they haven't been frozen or packed in any kind of solution. While they should still be moist, with a sheen like a pearl, they won't be sitting in a pool of liquid as "wet" scallops might be. Dry scallops have a cleaner flavor and will develop a nice golden-brown crust when seared in a pan.

To make the cider brown butter, bring the cider to a boil in a medium saucepan over high heat. Reduce it to approximately ½ cup, about 20 minutes. Meanwhile, in a small pan, melt the butter over low heat and simmer until it browns and develops a nutty aroma. Pour the browned butter into the reduced cider and stir to combine. Keep the sauce warm until ready to serve.

To make the Brussels sprouts, melt the butter in a medium sauté pan over high heat. When the butter foams, add the Brussels sprouts to the pan and sauté until lightly browned, about 10 minutes. Add the apples, cranberries, and cinnamon to the pan and cook until the apples are tender. Add the parsley and season to taste with salt. Hold the Brussels sprouts in a warm place until ready to serve.

Season the scallops with salt on both sides. Heat a generous coating of canola oil in a sauté pan over high heat. When the oil starts to smoke, carefully lay the scallops in the pan in a single layer. Reduce the heat to medium and sear the scallops until they're golden brown, about 2 minutes, then flip and sear the second side for 30 seconds.

To serve, spoon the Brussels sprouts onto warm plates and top with the seared scallops. Give the cider brown butter a brisk stir and spoon liberally over the scallops and around the plate. Garnish with the walnuts.

CRISPY SKATE WING

with Crab Bisque & Dirty Rice

For the Crab Bisque

2
COOKED JONAH CRABS

¼ cup
CANOLA OIL

1 cup
DICED ONION

2 cloves
GARLIC, smashed

1 cup
DICED CELERY

1 cup
DICED FENNEL

½ cup
DRY SHERRY

2 sprigs
THYME

1
BAY LEAF

½ teaspoon
CHILE FLAKES

½ teaspoon
SMOKED PAPRIKA

½ cup
FRESH OR CANNED CRUSHED TOMATOES

¼ cup
WHITE RICE (any kind)

4 cups
CHICKEN STOCK (page 17)

1 cup
HEAVY CREAM

For the Dirty Rice

2 tablespoons
UNSALTED BUTTER, at room temperature

2 tablespoons
CANOLA OIL

½ cup
SMALL-DICED LEEK

½ cup
SMALL-DICED GREEN BELL PEPPER

½ cup
SMALL-DICED CELERY

½ cup
SMALL-DICED FENNEL

1 cup
ARBORIO RICE

¼ cup
FRESH OR CANNED CRUSHED TOMATOES

4 cups
WATER, plus more if necessary

2 teaspoons
PAPRIKA

1 teaspoon
CHOPPED FRESH THYME

FINE SEA SALT

½
LEMON

In Louisiana and other parts of the Deep South, "dirty rice" is cooked with chicken liver and/or giblets along with the Cajun "trinity"—bell peppers, onions, and celery. This version, made from seafood, gets its "dirty" from the tomalley (guts) of the Jonah crab. The leftover bisque will hold well in the freezer for the day when you need a beautiful bowl of soup.

For the Skate Wing

4
SKATE WING FILLETS
(about 1½ pounds total)

1 cup
CORNMEAL

1 cup
RICE FLOUR

2 teaspoons
FINE SEA SALT,
plus more to taste

CANOLA OIL,
for sautéing

PAPRIKA,
for garnish

1
LEMON,
sliced into rounds, for garnish

CRAB BISQUE

Working over a bowl, cut away the top shell from the crabs and scrape out the green tomalley and liquid. Crack the crabs and remove the meat from the claws, back fins, knuckles, and bodies. Add the crabmeat to the bowl with the tomalley, cover, and refrigerate for the dirty rice. You'll use the crab bodies and shells for the bisque.

On a sturdy cutting board, gently crush the crab bodies and shells with a mallet or pan. In a medium stockpot, heat the oil over high heat until smoking. Scrape the crushed crab bodies and shells from the cutting board into the pot and cook for a few minutes, stirring frequently to prevent sticking. Add the onion, garlic, celery, and fennel to the pan and reduce the heat to low. Cook, stirring frequently, until the vegetables become soft and translucent, 10 to 12 minutes. Deglaze the pan with the dry sherry. Add all the remaining bisque ingredients except the heavy cream. Bring the pot just to a boil, then reduce the heat and simmer for 30 minutes. Pour in the heavy cream, bring the pot back to a boil, then remove it from the heat.

Recipe Continues

Carefully transfer the contents of the pot to a blender. To avoid splashing the hot liquid, fill the blender no more than halfway (blend in batches if necessary), then remove the center piece from the lid and hold a kitchen towel firmly over the hole as you blend. Pulse the bisque until smooth, then pass it through a fine-mesh sieve back into the pot. Warm the bisque over medium heat before serving or cool quickly in a metal container over an ice bath, cover, and refrigerate. The bisque may be made a day in advance.

DIRTY RICE

While the bisque is cooking, in a food processor, combine the butter with the reserved crabmeat and tomalley. Process until smooth. Cover the crab butter and refrigerate.

Heat the canola oil in a medium saucepan over medium heat. Gently sauté the leek, bell pepper, celery, and fennel, stirring frequently, until the vegetables are soft, 10 to 12 minutes. Add the Arborio rice to the pot and stir for a few minutes, until the rice becomes translucent. Pour in the crushed tomatoes and simmer until the excess liquid has evaporated. Add the water, paprika, and thyme. Bring to a boil,

stirring constantly, until most of the liquid has been absorbed, about 20 minutes. Taste a few grains of rice; they should still be firm but cooked through. If necessary, pour in additional water, ½ cup at a time, and simmer until the rice is cooked. The finished rice should be tighter and drier than a risotto. Remove the pan from the heat and stir in the crab butter. Season to taste with salt and a squeeze of lemon juice.

SKATE WING

Cut the skate wing fillets in half. Mix the cornmeal, rice flour, and salt in a shallow dish. Dredge the skate wing fillets in the flour mixture, thoroughly coating both sides.

Heat ¼ inch of canola oil in a large sauté pan over high heat. Once the oil is hot but not smoking, pan-fry the skate wing fillets until golden and crispy, about 2 minutes on each side. Work in batches if necessary. Transfer the skate to a plate lined with paper towels to drain, and season lightly with salt.

TO SERVE

Ladle ¼ cup of warm crab bisque into four broad bowls. Top with a large spoonful of dirty rice and two pieces of skate wing. Sprinkle the skate with paprika and garnish with slices of lemon.

AT THE FISH MARKET

With seafood, it's wise to start your meal planning at the market and then adapt an appropriate recipe to the best fish or shellfish you can find. Ask your fishmonger what's good that day, and check for freshness. Shellfish should be closed, or should close quickly when you tap their shells. Whole fish should have clear eyes and red gills. Fish fillets should be moist, not dry. Most importantly, fresh fish and shellfish should smell *clean*. A fishy-smelling fish is not fresh. At best, it may not taste yummy; at worst, it may be unsafe to eat.

GRILLED
BLUEFISH

WITH

Cranberry Bean & Linguiça Stew

2 cups
**FRESH CRANBERRY
BEANS** *OR*
1½ cups
DRIED BEANS

5 cups
WATER

3 small
**RED BLISS
POTATOES**

2 tablespoons
**EXTRA-VIRGIN
OLIVE OIL,**
plus more for drizzling

1
FENNEL BULB,
thinly sliced, green fronds
reserved for garnish

½ small
ONION,
sliced

2 cloves
GARLIC,
sliced

8 ounces
LINGUIÇA,
sliced ¼ inch thick

½ cup
**DICED OVEN-DRIED
TOMATOES**
(page 16)

1 small bunch
KALE,
cleaned and chopped

FINE SEA SALT

CANOLA OIL,
for the grill

4 (8-ounce)
BLUEFISH FILLETS,
skin on

2
LEMONS,
halved

Bluefish are in season and plentiful year-round in New York's fishing grounds. Lucky for us! This rich, flavorful fish pairs well with bold ingredients like linguiça, the traditional Portuguese smoked sausage. If you happen to be in Rhode Island, linguiça can be found at any supermarket. If you can't find any near you, pick some up online at GasparsSausage.com. (In a pinch, you can use chorizo instead, but be sure it's the cured Spanish type rather than the fresh Mexican type.)

In a medium saucepan, bring the fresh cranberry beans and water just to a boil over medium-high heat. Reduce the heat and simmer until the beans are tender, about 20 minutes. (If using dried beans, follow the supplier's directions for overnight soaking, amount of water, and cooking time.) Don't drain the beans after cooking; that liquid is part of the stew.

Meanwhile, fill a small saucepan with water and boil the potatoes over medium heat until tender, about 20 minutes. Drain the potatoes and slice them ¼ inch thick.

In a stockpot large enough to hold the entire stew, heat the olive oil over medium heat. Sauté the fennel, onion, and garlic, stirring frequently, until the vegetables are tender and translucent, 10 to 12 minutes. Pour the cranberry beans and their cooking liquid into the pot and bring it to a simmer. Add the potatoes, linguiça, dried tomatoes, and kale and simmer gently for another 5 minutes. Season with salt to taste.

Preheat the grill on high heat. Use a kitchen towel lightly coated with canola oil to season the grill when you're ready to cook the bluefish.

Salt the fillets on both sides and lay them on the grill, skin side down. Once the skin is crispy, about 6 minutes, flip the fillets and cook them on the other side for another minute or so, until they're cooked through. While the fish is cooking, char the cut sides of the lemon halves on the grill.

To serve, ladle the stew into wide, shallow bowls, making a mound of beans and vegetables in the middle. Lay a piece of fish on top of the stew. Garnish with a drizzle of olive oil, the reserved fennel fronds, and the grilled lemon halves.

Note: *A cast-iron grill pan works great for this recipe if an outdoor grill isn't an option. If you're cooking indoors, make sure to open some windows, because it's going to get smoky.*

HOW TO STORE FISH

*The challenge with storing fresh fish at home is that your
refrigerator just isn't cold enough. Most fish are perfectly comfortable
swimming in below-freezing waters, and the microbes
that live on them are acclimatized to those conditions as well.
Your 40-degree home refrigerator is like a balmy day to fish germs.
In order to slow their growth and keep fish safe and good
to eat, you need to pack them in ice, taking care not to soak their
delicate flesh. Here's how.*

Fin Fish

Whole fish and fillets should be stored in your refrigerator, nestled in a
bed of crushed ice. To allow the meltwater to drain, put the crushed ice in
a perforated pan on top of a second, nonperforated pan. (Perforated and
nonperforated "hotel pans" are available online and at any restaurant supply
store.) You can also improvise with a colander inside a bowl. A whole round
fish should be stored unwrapped and upright (the way they swim), belly side
in the ice. This position allows the fish to drain through its cavity. Fish fillets
should be wrapped in plastic or sealed freezer bags to protect them from
direct contact with the ice.

Shellfish

Live clams, oysters, and mussels need oxygen, so store them in an open container covered with a clean, damp towel to keep them from drying out. Before cooking, sort through the shellfish and discard any with open shells that don't close quickly after you give them a little tap or squeeze. Live lobsters should be held in a ventilated container, with some damp newspaper or seaweed to keep them moist.

PART THREE

GRILLED WHOLE PORGY

WITH GREEN TOMATO SAUCE VIERGE

Serves 2

2 large
GREEN TOMATOES

½ cup
EXTRA-VIRGIN OLIVE OIL

½ teaspoon
FENNEL SEEDS

1 small
SHALLOT,
diced small

1 tablespoon
CAPERS

GRATED ZEST OF ½ LEMON

4 teaspoons
SLICED SCALLION

2
LARGE BASIL LEAVES,
sliced

¼ cup
LIME JUICE

1
LARGE WHOLE PORGY
(about 1½ to 2 pounds), scaled and
gutted

CANOLA OIL,
for brushing

FINE SEA SALT

Porgy is one of the treasures of the Long Island and New England coasts, where it's responsibly fished and remains abundant. It's sweet and mild, with flaky white meat and skin that holds up well to grilling. This variation on the classic French *sauce vierge* substitutes green tomatoes for red, adding texture and zingy acidity.

To make the green tomato *sauce vierge*, first make a *concassé* from the green tomatoes (see box, right).

Combine the olive oil, fennel seeds, and shallot in a small saucepan and cook gently over medium-low heat. If the shallot starts to brown, reduce the heat. Once the shallot is soft, remove the pan from the heat and transfer the contents to a mixing bowl to cool for a few minutes. Add the green tomato *concassé*, capers, lemon zest, scallion, basil, and lime juice and stir to combine.

Preheat a grill or cast-iron grill pan over high heat. Very lightly brush the porgy with canola oil, season liberally with salt on all sides, and lay the fish on the grill. To keep the skin intact, resist the temptation to touch the fish until it has a nice char on it, 3 to 5 minutes. Flip the fish and cook until the second side is golden brown and crispy, 2 to 3 minutes.

Transfer the porgy to a serving platter. Pour half of the *sauce vierge* directly over the fish and serve the remainder on the side.

TOMATO CONCASSÉ

Bring a large saucepan or stockpot of water to a boil and prepare an ice water bath. Using a paring knife, score a small, shallow X on the bottom of each tomato (the end opposite the stem). Drop the tomatoes in the boiling water for about a minute, until the skins start to peel away from the edges of your Xs. Using a slotted spoon or skimmer, transfer the tomatoes to the ice water bath to cool for 3 minutes. Peel off the skin using your fingers or the edge of a paring knife. If the skin doesn't come away easily, give the tomatoes another 30-second trip through the boiling water and back to the ice water bath. After peeling, cut each tomato into four wedges. Lay each wedge, seed-side up, on the cutting board and cut away the seeds and core. Cut the wedges into a small dice.

BENTON'S
HAM-WRAPPED
TROUT

with Mustardy Mustard Greens

**4
LEEKS,**
white and tender green parts
only, washed and thinly sliced

**½ cup
WATER**

**1 tablespoon
UNSALTED BUTTER**

FINE SEA SALT

**2
RAINBOW TROUT,**
butterflied

**8 thin slices
BENTON'S COUNTRY
HAM**

CANOLA OIL,
for sautéing

**1 pound
MUSTARD GREENS,**
cut into 1-inch pieces

**2 tablespoons
DIJON MUSTARD**

**2 tablespoons
WHOLE-GRAIN
MUSTARD**

**¼ cup
CRÈME FRAÎCHE**

Rainbow trout are almost always sold butterflied (with the center bone removed), making them easy to stuff and serve whole. Benton's is a country ham, dry-cured and aged in Tennessee. If you can't find Benton's or another American country ham, serrano ham or prosciutto will work just fine. At Buttermilk Channel, we serve this fish on top of a mound of warm, creamy Grits (page 210).

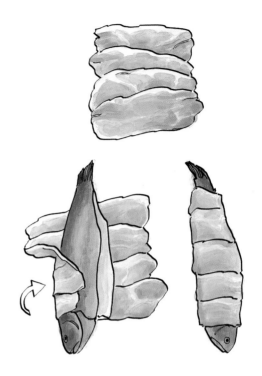

In a medium saucepan, combine the leeks with the water and butter and cook over medium-low heat until they are soft and tender, 10 to 12 minutes. Season with salt to taste and transfer to a plate or bowl to cool, uncovered, in the refrigerator while you prepare the trout.

If you don't want to look at them while you eat, cut the heads and tails off the trout. Otherwise, leave them intact. Remove the pin bones from the trout with fish tweezers. Spoon half of the cooked leeks into the cavity of each fish and fold it closed. Lay 4 slices of the ham, slightly overlapping, on a cutting board. Place one stuffed trout in the center of the ham and wrap it around the fish. Press the fish firmly into a tight package. Repeat with the remaining ham and second trout.

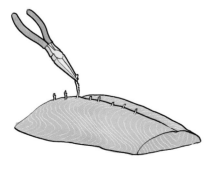

Preheat your oven to 350°F. In a nonstick sauté pan with a light coating of canola oil, sear the trout over medium heat until crispy, about 2 minutes per side. (Work in batches if necessary. If your pan is too small for a whole fish, cut them in half crosswise with a sharp knife before sautéing.) Transfer the trout to a baking dish and roast for 10 minutes, or until the fish is cooked through.

Return the nonstick pan to medium heat, pour in another light coating of canola oil, and sauté the mustard greens until tender. Transfer the mustard greens to a mixing bowl, toss with the mustards and crème fraîche, and season with salt to taste. Divide the greens among two or four plates, top with the trout (cut each in half crosswise if serving four people), and serve.

PARSLEY-CRUSTED
HAKE

with Summer Beans

1 pound
MIXED FRESH
SUMMER BEANS
(such as haricots verts, fava
beans, cranberry beans, or
Chinese long beans), trimmed

1 cup
PITTED GREEN
CASTELVETRANO
OR OTHER
GREEN OLIVES

¼ cup
EXTRA-VIRGIN
OLIVE OIL

¼ cup
PICKLED CHERRY
PEPPERS,
plus 2 tablespoons vinegar
from the jar

1 cup
FRESH FLAT-LEAF
PARSLEY LEAVES

1 cup
DRY BREAD CRUMBS

2 cloves
GARLIC,
smashed

1 tablespoon
GOLDEN RAISINS

4 (6-ounce)
HAKE FILLETS

FINE SEA SALT

CANOLA OIL,
for sautéing

½ cup
FRESH BASIL LEAVES,
torn

4 ounces
BABY LETTUCE
LEAVES
(like baby romaine, Bibb,
or Little Gem)

¼ cup
THINLY SHAVED
RED ONION

Serves 4

This dish visits the Buttermilk Channel menu every summer, when our farmers' markets are loaded with fresh beans. The olives and pickled cherry peppers create a flavor grand slam—sweet, salty, sour, bitter, umami.

Bring a large saucepan or stockpot of generously salted water to a boil over high heat and prepare a large ice water bath. Blanch the summer beans until they're cooked through but still firm. If you are using an assortment of beans, blanch each variety separately. Cool the beans in the ice water bath, then drain and set aside.

Chop the olives finely, almost into a paste, and mix with the olive oil. Set aside. Chop the cherry peppers into the same fine consistency, mix with the vinegar, and set aside.

Preheat your oven to 350°F. Combine the parsley, bread crumbs, garlic, and golden raisins in a food processor and process thoroughly. Transfer to a shallow bowl. Season the hake fillets with salt to taste. Press the fish into the parsley bread crumbs to coat on all sides.

Heat ¼ inch of canola oil in a large, oven-safe sauté pan over medium-high heat. When the oil is hot but not smoking, add the hake fillets and cook until golden brown on one side, 2 to 3 minutes. Carefully flip the fish and transfer the pan to the oven to roast for 8 to 10 minutes, until the fish is cooked through (see note).

To serve, reheat the beans in about ¼ cup of water in a small saucepan over high heat until hot. Drain any water that hasn't cooked off and transfer the beans to a mixing bowl. Gently toss the beans with the chopped olives, basil, lettuce leaves, and shaved onion. Divide the beans among four plates, spoon the cherry pepper and vinegar mixture over them, and top with the hake.

Note: *When hake, or any fish, is cooked through, a sharp paring knife will meet no resistance when inserted into the thickest part of the flesh.*

FLOUNDER
GRENOBLOISE

1 cup
**SMALL
CAULIFLOWER
FLORETS**

1 tablespoon
CANOLA OIL

FINE SEA SALT

1 (2- to 2½-pound)
WHOLE FLOUNDER,
prepared per headnote

1 cup
ALL-PURPOSE FLOUR

4 tablespoons (½ stick)
UNSALTED BUTTER

2 teaspoons
CAPERS

1
SHALLOT,
thinly sliced

1
BLOOD ORANGE,
cut into suprêmes
(see page 71)

1
LEMON,
cut into suprêmes
(see page 71)

1 tablespoon
**CHOPPED FRESH
FLAT-LEAF PARSLEY**

¼ cup
**SMALL TOASTED
CROUTONS**
made from brioche

Serves 2

This combination of brown butter, capers, citrus, and croutons is one of the greatest fish accompaniments ever devised. There isn't much evidence that it originated in the French city of Grenoble, but it is a preparation that any town would be proud to call its own (unlike tomato-based clam chowder, which New Englanders punted to Manhattan because they knew it sucked). Ask your fishmonger to prepare the whole flounder, removing the fins, head, and skin but leaving the fish on the bone.

Preheat your oven to 350°F. Toss the cauliflower in a bowl with the canola oil and salt to taste and spread out in a single layer on a rimmed baking sheet. Roast until tender, about 15 minutes.

Season the fish on both sides with salt to taste. Pour the flour onto a plate or shallow baking dish. Press both sides of the fish into the flour and gently shake off the excess, leaving a thin coating.

In a large sauté pan, heat 2 tablespoons of the butter over medium heat until it begins to brown. Lay the flounder in the hot butter and give the pan a quick shake to prevent it from sticking. Cook the fish for 3 minutes, then carefully flip. Add the remaining 2 tablespoons of butter to the pan and turn up the heat to high. With a large spoon, baste the fish with the browning butter for another 3 minutes, or until the fish is cooked through (see note, page 109). Transfer the fish to a serving platter.

Return the pan to medium heat and add the capers and shallot. Cook for 10 seconds, then add the citrus suprêmes, roasted cauliflower florets, and parsley. Cook for another few seconds to warm the garnish, then spoon the sauce liberally over the fish. Scatter the croutons over the top and serve.

PORTUGUESE-STYLE
PORK
& CLAMS

¼ cup
CANOLA OIL

FINE SEA SALT

1 pound
PORK TENDERLOIN,
cut into stew-size chunks

2 cloves
GARLIC,
chopped

¼ cup
DICED ONION

½ cup
**SLICED ROASTED RED
PEPPERS**

3 tablespoons
ANCHO CHILE PURÉE
(page 5)

12
LITTLENECK CLAMS

1 cup
**BOTTLED
CLAM JUICE**

1 cup
**LARGE-DICED SOUR
PICKLES**

1 pound
RED BLISS POTATOES,
diced

8 ounces
**LINGUIÇA OR
CURED CHORIZO**
(see page 101), sliced into thick
rounds

3 cups
WATER

2 cups
JULIENNED KALE

½ cup
PARSLEY PISTOU
(page 10)

**LOAF OF CRUSTY
BREAD,**
for serving

The inspiration for this stew is *carne de porco à alentejana*, one of Portugal's most traditional meals. Variations on this dish are found in Portuguese restaurants all over New England and New Jersey. The deep, rich, mild heat in this dish is yet another reason to keep ancho chile purée in your fridge.

Heat the canola oil in a heavy-bottomed sauté pan or Dutch oven over medium heat. Salt the pork well and brown in the oil (in batches, if necessary, to avoid steaming the meat in a crowded pot). Remove the pork from the pan using a slotted spoon and transfer to a plate. Add the garlic and onion to the pan and cook, stirring frequently, until the onion is soft and translucent, about 5 minutes. Add the roasted peppers and chile purée and cook, stirring, for another minute. Add the clams, clam juice, diced pickles, potatoes, linguiça, and water. Bring the pot to a boil and cover it.

When all the clams have opened, use a slotted spoon to transfer them to a bowl. Add the kale to the pan and cook, covered, until the kale has relaxed and the potatoes are soft, 10 to 15 minutes. Return the pork and clams to the pot and bring it back a simmer. Add salt, if needed, and serve immediately alongside a bowl of the parsley pistou and plenty of fresh, crusty bread.

AT THE DOOR

Walking through the front door of a restaurant can make you feel like the new kid in town on the first day of school. You're hoping for a warm welcome but afraid you won't fit in. A first glance at the staff and customers and your worries are confirmed—you're too young or too old, not cool enough or rich enough, and no one in the room looks like you. You brace yourself for rejection. Will it be "fully committed," or the equally forbidding "my next table for four is in three hours"? Are all the tables *really* full or do they just not like you?

When you come through the doors of French Louie, Ellen Simpson takes aim at your worries with a "y'all" straight to the heart.

You've got to be from the South to say "y'all," which is kind of unfair because we could all use that weapon in our arsenal. "Y'all" is one and a half syllables that hug you.

Ellen works the room, flitting about with brisk energy and Southern charm. She's delighted to see you, and her "Come in, y'all" is an order, not a request. It's accompanied by a rapid whisking motion she makes with her hands. She appears to be stirring up some kind of vortex to draw you into the room.

Ellen is the boss of a busy restaurant, but she acts as if she's inviting you onto her porch for a glass of cold lemonade. She makes you feel that you're the one who's busy, and she's insisting you make time for a quick visit.

If things are going your way, Ellen will slide you into a banquette and let your waiter take over. On another day the tables may be filled, and there may be a bit of a wait. If so, she'll drop you onto a bar stool for a glass of wine, or take your number and point you to a coffee shop or a cute store up the block. Maybe you can wait; maybe your appetite or movie tickets will send you elsewhere for a meal. Either way you'll know you've found a place where you're welcome.

At Buttermilk Channel, Jennifer Nelson greets you with a distinctly Northern charm. While Ellen flits, Jennifer serenely glides. She favors flowing, diaphanous garments that accentuate this illusion. Jennifer's a redhead—a good witch—and her gentle smile conveys a premonition happily confirmed. She's been looking forward to seeing you, and here you are.

Jennifer's serenity is at odds with the scene behind her. The room is bonkers. Waiters weave through tables, the bar is packed, and there's a bunch of people waiting for tables already. There doesn't appear to be a place for you, and yet she beckons you in.

Jennifer's calm under stress is impressive, but her superpower is the ability to transcend the physical reality of tables and chairs. In an ideal world, we'd get to say yes to everyone, whether they reserve two months in advance or walk in at eight o'clock on a Saturday night. Of course, that just isn't possible. *Or is it?* When Jennifer is at the door, no one seems to get "no" for an answer. You brought seven friends and a service dog? No problem. And a sleeping baby in a stroller? We'll find a spot. The next thing you know, the tables have spun into new configurations, your group is seated, the dog has water, and cocktails are on the way.

The word "restaurant" comes from the French verb *restaurer*: to restore. It's our job to return you to the world feeling better than when you walked in. We've succeeded if you leave not just with a full belly, but with the contentment that comes from being cared for—and maybe even spoiled a little.

In the process, we might become friends. Which means that the next time Ellen or Jennifer greets you, you won't feel like the new kid in town anymore.

Recipes

FOR

CHICKEN DUCK TURKEY PORK LAMB BEEF

4

BIRDS

AND

BEASTS

EVERYTHING IN MODERATION, including moderation," as Oscar Wilde (might have) said.

Like most people, we're eating meat differently—less of it, and better quality when we do—and we pride ourselves on offering a satisfying variety of vegetarian and pescatarian options at our restaurants. That said, bistros are an essentially carnivorous species. Ask us to help you decide between fried chicken and a salad, and we're going to nudge you gently in the direction of the thing we know you really want. Call us meat enablers—but when you want a steak, you want a steak.

Our places are neighborhood restaurants, and we see many of our friends and neighbors a few times a week. On Saturday night, they may splurge on a dry-aged rib eye, but on Tuesday, they want a hunk of meat that won't break the bank. To satisfy those customers, we draw upon another bistro tradition: the use of old-fashioned techniques for transforming humbler cuts into luxurious feasts.

COOKING
STEAKS FOR A
PARTY 162

BROWNING MEAT
FOR BRAISING 147

SETTING THE
STAGE
166

CHICORY COFFEE-RUBBED QUAIL KEBABS WITH CHERRY PEPPER JELLY 122

CHICKEN LIVER PÂTÉ 124

STEAK TARTARE 125

CAST-IRON ROASTED CHICKEN WITH BELUGA LENTILS, SUNCHOKES & WALNUT VINAIGRETTE 126

BUTTERMILK FRIED CHICKEN WITH CHEDDAR WAFFLES & BALSAMIC-SPIKED MAPLE SYRUP 128

DUCK MEATLOAF 134

ROAST DUCK LEGS ALLARD WITH CASTELVETRANO OLIVES, FENNEL POLLEN & DUCK JUS 136

DUCK BREAST AU POIVRE WITH BLOOD ORANGE MARMALADE & BABY TURNIP CONFIT 138

BRAISED LAMB NECK
WITH SPRING PEAS, OMELET & PISTOU 140

SLOW-ROASTED PORK SPARE RIBS
WITH ANCHO CHILE MARINADE 143

BRAISED SHORT RIBS
WITH FRIED LEMON & ANCHOVY MASH 144

LAMB BLADE CHOPS WITH CHARRED SUGAR
SNAP PEAS & WARM ANCHOVY VINAIGRETTE 148

BOEUF BOURGUIGNON
"À LA MINUTE" 150

DINDE AU VIN
(TURKEY BRAISED IN RED WINE WITH PORK BELLY & MUSHROOMS) 152

LAMB CLUB SANDWICH 154

STEAK FRITES 156

WINE 169

CHEESE 173

CHICORY COFFEE–RUBBED

QUAIL KEBABS

with Cherry Pepper Jelly

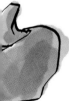

4
SEMI-BONELESS QUAIL

½ cup
GROUND CHICORY COFFEE OR REGULAR GROUND COFFEE

½ cup
loose-packed
DARK BROWN SUGAR

¼ cup
FINE SEA SALT

2
RED BELL PEPPERS,
seeded and finely chopped

1
GREEN BELL PEPPER,
seeded and finely chopped

10
CHERRY PEPPERS,
seeded and finely chopped

1 cup
APPLE CIDER VINEGAR

1 (1.75-ounce) package
POWDERED PECTIN

1 tablespoon
BLACK PEPPER

5 cups
GRANULATED SUGAR

Special Equipment

8 (6-inch)
BAMBOO SKEWERS

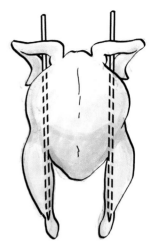

This quail is a favorite on the annual New Year's Eve menu at Buttermilk Channel. Quail is available at most butcher shops and is generally sold semi-boneless, with the breast- and backbones removed. This makes for easy skewering and quick, even grilling. Chocolaty-toasty chicory blends seamlessly with the charred flavors that come from a hot grill, but you can use regular coffee if chicory is unavailable.

Soak the bamboo skewers in water for 20 minutes to minimize burning.

Lay the quail on a flat surface, breast side up. Insert one skewer through the top of the right half of the breast and push it down through the length of the leg, keeping close to the bone. Ideally, the point of the skewer will be at the end of the drumstick. Repeat with a second skewer on the left half of the quail. (See illustration above.) Repeat the process for each quail.

In a small bowl, combine the coffee, brown sugar, and salt. Rub each quail with a generous amount of this mixture. Refrigerate the quail, uncovered, for at least a couple of hours or overnight.

Meanwhile, combine the chopped peppers, vinegar, pectin, and black pepper in a large saucepan and bring to a boil over medium heat, stirring constantly. Pour in the granulated

sugar and return to a boil, continuing to stir. Let boil for 1 minute. Remove from the heat, cool to room temperature, and refrigerate in a covered container (see note).

When ready to cook, preheat a grill or a cast-iron grill pan over high heat. Grill the quail for 3 to 4 minutes on each side and transfer to a cutting board.

To serve, cut each quail in half down the center of the breast so that you get two quail kebabs from each bird. Warm about 1 cup of the pepper jelly in a small saucepan over low heat and dollop some on each plate or serve on the side.

Note: *This recipe makes about 6 cups of jelly, more than you'll need for the quail. The jelly will last almost indefinitely in an airtight container in the refrigerator, or you can jar it following normal canning procedures.*

CHICKEN LIVER PÂTÉ

8 tablespoons (1 stick)
UNSALTED BUTTER

1 pound
CHICKEN LIVERS

2
SHALLOTS,
chopped

½ large
CARROT,
chopped

1
APPLE,
peeled, cored, and cut into
1-inch chunks

1½ teaspoons
FINE SEA SALT,
plus more to taste

¼ cup
CALVADOS OR APPLEJACK

¼ cup
HEAVY CREAM

Makes about 3 cups

You can't make a silk purse from a sow's ear, but you can make a luxurious pâté from one of the humblest—and cheapest—parts of a chicken. Spread thickly on toast with a sprinkle of chives on top, this pâté will be the star of your picnic, or the most popular canapé at the party.

Cut 5 tablespoons of the butter into ½-inch cubes and chill in the refrigerator. Leave the remaining 3 tablespoons out for cooking. Rinse the livers and pat dry between a few layers of paper towel.

Melt 1½ tablespoons of the butter in a medium sauté pan over high heat. Sauté the shallots and carrot until they're soft and lightly caramelized, about 10 minutes. Add the apple chunks and cook until they become soft, then carefully scrape the mixture into a food processor or blender.

Return the pan to medium heat and add the remaining 1½ tablespoons butter. When the butter begins to brown, sear the livers, tossing the pan to brown them on all sides. Season the livers with the salt. Remove the pan from the stove and pour in the Calvados, then return the pan to medium heat and shake to ignite the alcohol. Cook, stirring carefully, until the flame burns out. Scrape the contents of the pan into the food processor with the apple mixture.

Pour the heavy cream into the food processor and blend, adding the chilled butter a few chunks at a time. Continue blending until all the butter is incorporated. Taste and add more salt if necessary. For a smoother pâté, push the warm mixture through a fine-mesh sieve with a spatula before chilling.

Transfer the warm pâté to a serving bowl or ramekins and refrigerate, uncovered, for about 2 hours, until it's chilled and set. The pâté will keep for up to a week covered in the refrigerator.

STEAK TARTARE

Makes 4 appetizer-size servings

The leanest cuts of beef, like tenderloin, chuck, or flatiron, are best for tartare. This version (a year-round staple on the menu at French Louie) gets a vibrant pop from crunchy pickled mustard seeds. Warm, salty pommes frites (page 164) and a simple salad are the perfect accompaniments, along with plenty of fresh, crusty bread.

Combine the chopped beef, mustard seeds, pistou, and chile oil in a mixing bowl. Season with salt to taste. Divide equally among four chilled plates and top each serving with an egg yolk. Place 1 tablespoon of cornichons on each plate and serve.

**8 ounces
LEAN BEEF,**
coarsely chopped

**1 tablespoon
PICKLED MUSTARD SEEDS**
(see page 31)

**1 tablespoon
PARSLEY PISTOU**
(see page 10)

**2 tablespoons
CHILE OIL**

FINE SEA SALT

**4
LARGE EGG YOLKS**

**4 tablespoons
CHOPPED CORNICHONS**

CAST–IRON ROASTED CHICKEN

WITH BELUGA LENTILS, SUNCHOKES & WALNUT VINAIGRETTE

1 (2- to 3-pound)
FREE-RANGE CHICKEN
(Ask your butcher to prepare the chicken so you have two boneless halves with the wings, bone in, attached.)

CANOLA OIL,
for sautéing

FINE SEA SALT

8 ounces
SUNCHOKES,
peeled and diced small

1 cup
BELUGA LENTILS

1½ cups
WATER

½ cup
BALSAMIC VINEGAR

1
BAY LEAF

1 tablespoon
UNSALTED BUTTER

1 tablespoon
WHOLE-GRAIN MUSTARD

¼ cup
CHOPPED TOASTED WALNUTS
(see page 49)

¾ cup
CARAMELIZED CHICKEN JUS
(page 18)

¼ cup
WALNUT OIL

2 tablespoons
SHERRY VINEGAR

Special Equipment

1
BRICK OR OTHER WEIGHT
(see headnote), washed and wrapped in aluminum foil

Cooking chicken "under a brick" is a trick that cooks all over the world use to achieve that ideal combination of crispy skin and juicy meat. At French Louie we use a regular old brick, but the technique works with whatever appropriately sized brick-like weight you have on hand.

Preheat your oven to 400°F. In a cast-iron skillet, heat ⅛ inch of canola oil over medium-high heat until it's smoking. Season the boneless chicken halves (with wings attached) with salt and nestle them together, skin side down, in the pan. Sit the foil-wrapped brick on top of the chicken, turn the heat to medium-low, and cook until the skin is golden brown, about 6 minutes. Remove the brick, flip the chicken, and transfer the pan to the oven. Roast for about 10 minutes, until a kitchen thermometer reads 165°F when inserted into the thickest part of the meat.

Meanwhile, toss the sunchokes with a light coating of canola oil and spread them out in a single layer on a rimmed baking sheet. Roast until tender, about 15 minutes. In a medium saucepan, combine the lentils, water, vinegar, and bay leaf. Bring to a boil over medium heat, then reduce the heat and simmer for 20 minutes, or until the lentils are cooked through but still slightly chewy. Off the heat, whisk in the butter and mustard until combined, then stir in the walnuts and roasted sunchokes.

To serve, warm the chicken jus in a small saucepan. Spoon about a cup of the lentil mixture into two shallow bowls and lay the chicken halves on top. Whisk together the walnut oil and sherry vinegar with a fork and drizzle it over the chicken. Serve the warmed chicken jus on the side.

BUTTERMILK
FRIED
CHICKEN

WITH CHEDDAR WAFFLES
& BALSAMIC-SPIKED MAPLE SYRUP

For the Cheddar Waffles

3 cups
ALL-PURPOSE FLOUR

1 cup
CORNMEAL

¼ cup
SUGAR

2 tablespoons
BAKING POWDER

3 teaspoons
FINE SEA SALT

2½ cups
BUTTERMILK

1 cup
WHOLE MILK

6
LARGE EGGS

10 tablespoons
UNSALTED BUTTER,
melted

4 cups
**SHREDDED CHEDDAR
CHEESE**

For the Maple-Vinegar Syrup

1 cup
BALSAMIC VINEGAR

1 cup
MAPLE SYRUP

For the Fried Chicken

2 (2½- to 3-pound)
**FREE-RANGE
CHICKENS**

4 cups
BUTTERMILK

7 cups
ALL-PURPOSE FLOUR

2 tablespoons
FINE SEA SALT,
plus more to taste

2 tablespoons
BLACK PEPPER

4 quarts
CANOLA OIL

Special Equipment

**CANDY OR DEEP-FRY
THERMOMETER**

**BELGIAN WAFFLE
IRON**

Serves 4 to 6

Fried chicken is a powerful force, a thing that people obsess over, and crave all day long. Fortunately for our little restaurant in a far-flung corner of Brooklyn, it's also a dish people will travel for. At Buttermilk Channel, fried chicken outsells our other entrees three to one.

The world's eaters, from Seoul to Savannah, are all looking for the same qualities in their fried chicken: a crispy-crunchy crust surrounding juicy, tender meat. This recipe takes a few extra steps to ensure those desired results, and these steps do take some time and forethought, but we think they're worth it.

First, the chicken takes an overnight bath in buttermilk, which adds its tangy character while altering the meat to allow it to remain juicy. It rests again after it gets its flour coating, an interval that gives the flour and buttermilk time to form a more perfect union. Most importantly, the chicken must be fried twice, first at a lower temperature to cook the meat, and then at a higher temperature, bringing the crust to the desired crunchy, deep golden brown.

CHEDDAR WAFFLES

In a mixing bowl, whisk together the flour, cornmeal, sugar, baking powder, and salt. In another bowl, whisk together the buttermilk, milk, and eggs. Pour the wet ingredients into the dry and stir until completely integrated. Stir in the melted butter, then the cheddar. Cook the batter in an electric waffle iron following the manufacturer's instructions. Hold the waffles in a low oven until it's time to serve, or make them ahead of time and cool completely, then reheat in the oven or a toaster.

MAPLE-VINEGAR SYRUP

Pour the balsamic vinegar into a saucepan and simmer over medium heat to reduce by half, about 10 minutes. Stir in the maple syrup. Keep warm to serve.

FRIED CHICKEN

Cut each chicken in half with a sturdy knife or cleaver, discarding the backbones or saving for chicken stock (page 17). Separate the breasts from the legs. Cut the breasts in half across the middle, and cut the legs in half to separate the thighs and the drumsticks (see illustration, page 133). Your two chickens should yield 16 pieces total.

Recipe Continues

Put the chicken pieces in a large container and pour in the buttermilk, tossing so that all the pieces are coated. Cover the container with plastic wrap or a lid and leave the chicken to marinate in the refrigerator for 24 hours.

Combine the flour, salt, and pepper in a large bowl. Dust a rimmed baking sheet (large enough to hold all the chicken) with some of the seasoned flour. Remove the chicken pieces from the buttermilk one at a time and dredge them in the bowl of flour, coating them on all sides, then lay them out on the baking sheet. Wrap the pan tightly with plastic wrap and refrigerate the chicken for at least 1 hour or overnight. Cover the remaining flour mixture and refrigerate.

Pour the canola oil into an 8-quart stockpot and heat it over high heat until it registers 325°F on a candy thermometer (see note). Dredge four chicken pieces again in the reserved flour, shake off the excess, and carefully drop them, one at a time, into the hot oil. Using a slotted spoon, move the chicken pieces around to prevent them from sticking together. Fry the chicken until it's light golden brown, about 10 minutes, then use the slotted spoon to transfer the pieces to a baking sheet lined with paper towels. Repeat with the remaining chicken, dredging and frying in batches of four pieces.

Raise the temperature of the oil to 350°F. Fry the chicken again, in batches of four pieces at a time, until it reaches an internal temperature of 165°F, about 8 to 10 minutes depending on the size of your chicken pieces. Transfer the chicken to a baking sheet lined with fresh paper towels and salt immediately and thoroughly. The crust of this chicken does a great job of holding the heat in, so it will still be piping hot after 10 minutes at room temperature. If you need more time, you can hold the chicken in a low oven until you're ready to serve.

TO SERVE

Arrange the cheddar waffles on a platter and pile the fried chicken on top. Serve with the maple-vinegar syrup on the side.

Note: *An electric deep-fryer may be used for this recipe, following the manufacturer's instructions on how much oil to use and your own judgment on how much chicken can be fried in each batch.*

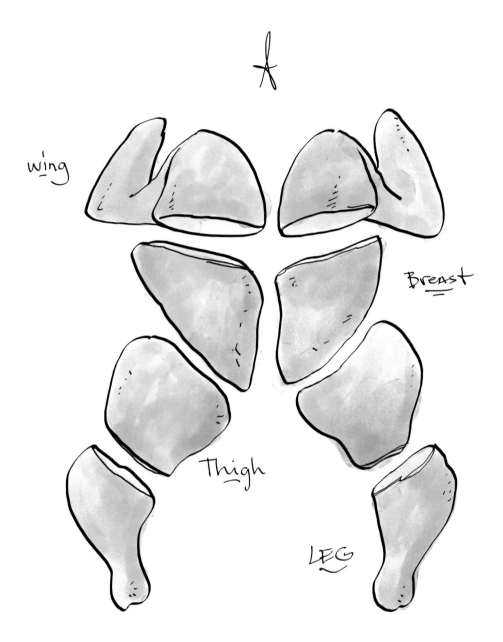

wing

Breast

Thigh

LEG

DUCK MEATLOAF

CANOLA OIL,
for sautéing

**1
SMALL ONION,**
finely diced

**1 (1-pound)
BONELESS PEKING
OR LONG ISLAND
DUCK BREAST,**
ground with the skin on (grind
it yourself or ask your butcher)

**¼ cup
BLACK RAISINS,**
very finely chopped (or passed
through the grinder with the
duck if you're grinding your
own meat)

**1
LARGE EGG,**
beaten

**½ cup
DRIED BREAD
CRUMBS**

**¼ cup
finely chopped
FRESH FLAT-LEAF
PARSLEY**

**1 teaspoon
finely chopped
FRESH THYME LEAVES**

**1½ teaspoons
FINE SEA SALT**

Serves 4

This dish has been a staple on the Buttermilk Channel menu since the day we opened. It starts out like a country pâté, then gets cooked like a hamburger—a French-American hybrid that would play in Paris or Peoria. The accompaniments for this dish have spanned the world as well—we've served it on top of everything from celery root purée to succotash and topped it, at various times, with onion rings, an apple salad, and blistered shishito peppers. Putting one on a bun with some mustard would not be a bad idea either.

Heat a thin coating of canola oil in a small sauté pan over medium heat. Sauté the onion slowly, until soft but not browned, then transfer to a large mixing bowl. While the onion cools to room temperature, preheat your oven to 325°F. Add the ground duck and all the remaining ingredients to the bowl with the cooled onion. Mix thoroughly with clean hands until all the ingredients are combined. Divide the mixture into four portions. Use a 3-inch diameter ring mold to shape the duck mixture into cylinders about 2 inches tall, or use your hands to form thick patties of approximately that shape and size.

Coat a large skillet with canola oil and sear one side of the meatloaves over medium heat for about 3 minutes. Flip the meatloaves and move the skillet to the oven. Cook for about 20 minutes, until they reach an internal temperature of 140°F (see note).

Remove the meatloaves from the pan and allow them to rest for 5 minutes before serving.

Note: *This meatloaf browns faster than a hamburger, so keep a close eye on the pan. If the crust looks like it will be too dark before the inside is cooked, transfer them to a new pan and put them back in the oven.*

ROAST
DUCK LEGS
ALLARD

*with Castelvetrano Olives, Fennel Pollen
& Duck Jus*

This is our homage to the *canard de Challans aux olives*, a whole roasted duck under a mountain of nutty green olives that's been on the menu at Allard in Paris for over eighty years. On a recent trip to New York, Allard's chef, Laetitia Rouabah, dropped by French Louie to inspect our version. Although we stray from the original by substituting user-friendly duck legs for a whole duck, she assured us that we've honored the spirit of the dish and granted us the Allard seal of approval. International culinary crisis averted.

In a small bowl, combine 2 tablespoons of the fennel pollen with the salt and season the duck legs liberally with this mixture. Arrange the duck legs in a single layer on a plate or rimmed baking sheet and refrigerate, uncovered, for 2 hours. Preheat your oven to 375°F. Transfer the duck legs to a rack set over a rimmed baking sheet and roast them for 45 minutes, or until they're golden brown and a thermometer inserted in the thickest part of the meat reads 165°F.

To serve, combine the olives, orange zest, and duck jus in a medium saucepan. Bring to a simmer over medium heat and reduce by half, about 10 minutes. Plate the duck legs in shallow bowls along with a generous amount of the duck jus. Surround each leg with about ½ cup of olives and garnish with the remaining 1 tablespoon of fennel pollen.

Note: *Fennel pollen has an intense and nuanced licorice flavor. It is available online or at specialty grocery stores.*

3 tablespoons
FENNEL POLLEN
(see note)

1 tablespoon
FINE SEA SALT

6
PEKING OR LONG ISLAND DUCK LEGS

4 cups
PITTED CASTELVETRANO OR OTHER GREEN OLIVES

GRATED ZEST OF 1 ORANGE

2 cups
DUCK JUS
(page 19)

DUCK BREAST
AU POIVRE

WITH

*Blood Orange Marmalade
& Baby Turnip Confit*

4
BLOOD ORANGES

½ cup
RED WINE VINEGAR

½ cup
SUGAR

2 bunches small
BABY TURNIPS,
greens trimmed and reserved

CANOLA OIL,
for cooking

1 tablespoon
**WHOLE BLACK
PEPPERCORNS**

1 tablespoon
**WHOLE SICHUAN
PEPPERCORNS**

1 tablespoon
**WHOLE PINK
PEPPERCORNS**

4
**BONELESS
PEKING
OR LONG ISLAND
DUCK BREASTS,**
skin on

FINE SEA SALT

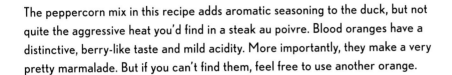

Serves 4

The peppercorn mix in this recipe adds aromatic seasoning to the duck, but not quite the aggressive heat you'd find in a steak au poivre. Blood oranges have a distinctive, berry-like taste and mild acidity. More importantly, they make a very pretty marmalade. But if you can't find them, feel free to use another orange.

Chop the oranges into 1-inch pieces, leaving the peel intact. In a medium saucepan, combine the chopped oranges, vinegar, and sugar. Simmer over low heat until the orange is soft and the liquid has reduced by half, about 10 minutes. Keep the blood orange marmalade at room temperature until ready to use (see note).

Put the turnips in a small saucepan and pour in enough canola oil to immerse them completely. Bring the oil to a gentle simmer over low heat and cook the turnips until they're tender, testing them after about 10 minutes. The tip of a paring knife should meet with no resistance. Remove the turnips from the pot with a slotted spoon and drain on a clean kitchen towel or a double layer of paper towels. The canola oil may be cooled and saved to be used again for sautéing vegetables.

Combine all the peppercorns in a spice grinder and grind coarsely. Season the duck breasts with salt and generously sprinkle the peppercorn mixture on all sides. Heat a seasoned cast-iron pan over medium-high heat until it starts to smoke. Pour a light coating of canola oil into the pan, turn the heat to low, and lay the duck breasts in the pan, skin side down. Cook slowly on the skin side until it's browned and crispy, 10 to 15 minutes. Flip the breasts and continue to cook for another 2 minutes for medium-rare or 4 minutes for medium. Transfer the duck to a plate or cutting board. Add the turnip greens to the duck fat and wilt over medium heat. Add the cooked turnips to the pan to reheat them, and season with salt to taste.

Cut the duck breasts in half lengthwise and divide them among four plates, along with the turnips and greens and a spoonful of the blood orange marmalade.

Note: *Store any leftover marmalade in an airtight container in the refrigerator for up to a week.*

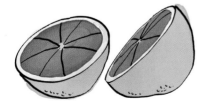

BRAISED LAMB NECK

WITH SPRING PEAS, OMELET & PISTOU

2 (2-pound)
BONE-IN LAMB NECKS

FINE SEA SALT

BLACK PEPPER

CANOLA OIL

1
LARGE CARROT,
roughly chopped

1
ONION,
roughly chopped

4 cloves
GARLIC,
smashed

2 cups
DRY WHITE WINE

6 cups
CHICKEN STOCK
(page 17)

2
BAY LEAVES

2 sprigs
THYME

8
LARGE EGGS

½ cup
GRATED PECORINO ROMANO CHEESE

1½ cups
ENGLISH PEAS

½ cup
PARSLEY PISTOU
(page 10)

Spitzad is an Italian peasant dish of lamb neck chunks on the bone, stewed with onion and garlic, and finished with scrambled eggs and grated Pecorino Romano. It was the main course of the first meal Ryan was served by his future mother-in-law, Mary. Lamb neck and scrambled eggs? It was a test and he passed. This fancier, Frenchified version, which transforms the scrambled eggs into a delicate omelet, makes an appearance on the French Louie menu every spring in honor of that first meal.

Preheat your oven to 400°F. Season the lamb necks with salt and pepper and place them on a rimmed baking sheet or roasting pan. Roast the necks for about 30 minutes, until they're golden brown, then remove from the oven. Leave the oven on.

Heat 2 tablespoons of canola oil in a large, heavy-bottomed, oven-safe stockpot or Dutch oven over medium heat. Sauté the carrot, onion, and garlic, stirring frequently, until the vegetables are lightly caramelized, about 8 minutes. Pour in the white wine and simmer to reduce by half, about 5 minutes.

Add the roasted lamb necks and chicken stock to the pot. The lamb necks should be just submerged in liquid; if the stock doesn't cover them, add a little water. Turn the heat to high and bring the pot just to a boil, then remove it from the heat. Add the bay leaves and thyme, cover with a lid, and move the pot to the oven. Immediately turn the oven down to 325°F. Cook the lamb for 2½ to 3 hours, until the meat is falling off the bone.

Transfer the lamb necks from the braising liquid to a clean dish and allow them to cool to room temperature. Using two forks or clean hands, gently remove the meat from the bones. Strain the braising liquid through a fine-mesh sieve, discarding the vegetables and herbs. Return the braising liquid to the pot and simmer over medium heat until reduced to 4 cups, about 10 minutes. Turn off the heat and add the lamb meat to the pot. Set aside until ready to serve.

To make the omelet, beat the eggs thoroughly with a fork or whisk, adding ½ teaspoon of salt as you whisk. Heat a small nonstick pan with a light coating of canola

Recipe Continues

oil over medium heat. Pour one-quarter of the scrambled eggs (about ¼ cup) into the pan and move the pan around until the entire surface is coated. Cook for about a minute, until the egg is set. Using a heatproof spatula, loosen the egg and slide it onto a clean work surface. Sprinkle the entire surface of the egg with 1 tablespoon of grated Pecorino Romano and roll it up like a cigar. Repeat with the remainder of the eggs, making a total of four omelets.

To serve, bring the stew to a simmer over medium heat. Taste and add salt if needed. Add the English peas and simmer until the peas are just tender, 2 to 3 minutes, then remove the pot from the heat. Divide the omelets among four shallow bowls. Spoon some meat and peas into the bowls and pour a few ounces of the braising liquid over everything. Top each bowl with a generous dollop of parsley pistou and 1 tablespoon of grated Pecorino Romano.

SLOW-ROASTED PORK SPARE RIBS

with Ancho Chile Marinade

Serves 4

This is basically Chinese char siu pork, adapted to the ingredients we have on hand in our kitchens. For a side-by-side comparison, grab an order of these ribs to-go from Buttermilk Channel, then cross the Manhattan Bridge (left onto the Bowery) and order the roast pork at Great NY Noodletown. We think our ribs give theirs a run for their money. But for roast Peking duck, Noodletown wins, hands down.

Combine the chile purée, vinegar, sugar, salt, and garlic in a blender and process until smooth. Pour about half of this mixture into a baking dish, add the ribs, and toss to coat them thoroughly. Cover the baking dish with aluminum foil and refrigerate overnight. Transfer the remainder of the marinade to an airtight container and refrigerate overnight.

Preheat your oven to 300°F. Roast the ribs, still covered with foil, for 3½ hours, or until the meat is falling off the bone. Remove the baking dish from the oven and turn the temperature up to 400°F. Brush the ribs with the reserved marinade and return them to the oven, uncovered, for 10 to 15 minutes. To serve, cut the rack into individual ribs or leave in hunks of 3 to 4 ribs each.

1 cup
ANCHO CHILE PURÉE
(page 5)

2 cups
APPLE CIDER VINEGAR

½ cup
SUGAR

6 tablespoons
FINE SEA SALT

18 cloves
GARLIC,
smashed

1 (3-pound)
RACK PORK SPARE RIBS

BRAISED

SHORT RIBS

WITH FRIED LEMON & ANCHOVY MASH

For the Short Ribs

8 (8-ounce)
BONE-IN SHORT RIBS

FINE SEA SALT

BLACK PEPPER

2 tablespoons
CANOLA OIL,
plus more for brushing

2
CARROTS,
chopped

1
SMALL ONION,
chopped

2 cloves
GARLIC,
smashed

¼ cup
RED WINE VINEGAR

1 (750 ml) bottle
DRY RED WINE

1
BAY LEAF

2 sprigs
THYME

1 strip
LEMON PEEL
(about 2 inches by 1 inch)

8 cups
CHICKEN STOCK
(page 17)

For the Anchovy Mash

2 pounds
YUKON GOLD
POTATOES

FINE SEA SALT

8
SALT-PACKED WHOLE
ANCHOVIES,
rinsed, boned, and chopped, *OR*
16 OIL-PACKED
ANCHOVY FILLETS,
drained and chopped

¾ cup
WHOLE MILK

¼ cup
EXTRA-VIRGIN
OLIVE OIL

For the Fried Lemons

16
THIN LEMON SLICES

½ cup
BUTTERMILK

CANOLA OIL,
for frying

1 cup
ALL-PURPOSE FLOUR

FINE SEA SALT

Braised short ribs are perfect for a wintertime dinner party. You can complete all the cooking a day (or several days) in advance, then all you have do when your guests come over is bring the pot to a simmer while you catch up over cocktails. If you do cook these ribs in advance, cool and store them right in their cooking liquid. If you're serving a smaller group, reserve the leftovers to make short rib hash for brunch (page 211).

SHORT RIBS

Preheat your oven to 400°F. Season the short ribs thoroughly with salt and pepper. Lightly brush them with oil and lay them on a rimmed baking sheet. Roast the short ribs until they are well browned, about 30 minutes. Leave the oven on.

Meanwhile, heat the oil in a heavy-bottomed pan or Dutch oven over medium heat. Add the carrots, onion, and garlic and cook, stirring frequently, until lightly caramelized, about 10 minutes. Pour in the vinegar and cook until it's completely absorbed. Add the red wine, bay leaf, thyme, and lemon peel and simmer to reduce the liquid by half, about 15 minutes.

Put the browned short ribs in the pot, cover with the chicken stock, and bring to a boil. Remove the pot from the heat and cover. Transfer the pot to the oven and immediately turn it down to 325°F. Cook until the short ribs are tender, about 2½ hours.

Remove the short ribs from the pot and strain the liquid through a fine-mesh sieve. Discard the vegetables and herbs and return the strained liquid to the pot. Gently simmer the braising liquid over low heat, skimming any fat and impurities, until it's reduced to 2 cups, about 20 minutes. Return the short ribs to the pot and cover. Set aside until ready to serve.

Recipe Continues

ANCHOVY MASH

Peel the potatoes and put them in a medium saucepan. Cover the potatoes with water and add a pinch of salt. Bring the water to a boil over medium heat, then lower the heat to a simmer and cook the potatoes until they're tender. Put the anchovies in a small saucepan and add the milk. Bring the milk to a boil over medium heat, then remove the pan from the stove and set aside.

Drain the cooked potatoes and transfer them to a standing mixer with the whisk attachment. Whisk the potatoes on low speed for a minute to allow some of the steam to escape. Slowly drizzle in the milk and anchovies and whisk for another minute. Turn the mixer up to medium and slowly drizzle in the olive oil. Taste the potatoes and add more salt if needed. Set aside.

FRIED LEMONS

Soak the lemon slices in the buttermilk for at least 5 minutes. Heat ¼ inch of canola oil in a large skillet over medium heat. One at a time, dredge the lemon slices in the flour and shake off any excess. Working in batches, fry the floured lemon slices in the oil until they're golden brown on both sides. Transfer the fried lemons to a plate lined with paper towels and season with salt while they're still hot.

TO SERVE

Scoop a generous mound of potatoes onto each plate, and lay the short ribs on top. Ladle some of the braising liquid around the plate and garnish with the fried lemons.

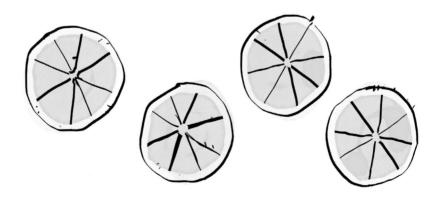

BROWNING MEAT FOR BRAISING

Recipes for stews and braises generally instruct the cook to sear meat on all sides before adding liquid and starting the low, slow cooking process. But when you sear in a pan, cooking one side at a time, you end up basically pan-frying the meat, filling your whole house with greasy smoke in the process.

Searing in a hot oven, which roasts the meat on all sides at once, is a more effective and cleaner way to get the job done. This technique works for everything from short ribs to chicken legs:

1. Season the meat.

2. Brush all sides of the meat with a light coating of oil.

3. Place the meat in a single layer on a rimmed baking sheet and roast in a 400°F oven until it's browned to your satisfaction.

4. Remove the meat from the pan and discard any excess oil.

5. While the pan is still hot, deglaze it with a cup or so of water or chicken stock, scraping the caramelized bits off the bottom with a wooden spoon. This can be added to your braising liquid for color and flavor.

LAMB BLADE CHOPS

*with Charred Sugar Snap Peas &
Warm Anchovy Vinaigrette*

**4 (12-ounce)
BONE-IN LAMB
BLADE CHOPS**

FINE SEA SALT

BLACK PEPPER

CANOLA OIL,
for sautéing

**1 pound
SUGAR SNAP PEAS,**
trimmed (see page 50)

**4 ounces
PEA SHOOTS**

**2 tablespoons thinly sliced
SPRING ONION
OR SCALLION**

**¼ cup
CELERY LEAVES**

**¼ cup
FRESH FLAT-LEAF
PARSLEY LEAVES**

**¼ cup
EXTRA-VIRGIN
OLIVE OIL**

**2
SALT-PACKED WHOLE
ANCHOVIES,**
rinsed and boned, *OR*
**4 OIL-PACKED
ANCHOVY FILLETS**

JUICE OF 1 LEMON

**⅔ cup
PARSLEY PISTOU**
(page 10)

The blade chop is a relatively thin steak, cut from the shoulder of the lamb. It's a far gutsier cut than a loin chop—rich and chewy (in a good way)—and similar in character to a leg chop, which would also work well for this recipe.

Season the lamb chops generously with salt and pepper. Heat a thin coating of canola oil in a cast-iron pan over high heat until it just begins to smoke. Cook the chops, flipping once, until they're medium-rare, 3 to 4 minutes on each side. (If necessary, use two pans or cook in batches to avoid crowding the pan.) Remove the chops from the pan and allow them to rest.

While the chops rest, wipe the pan clean and return it to high heat. Add the snap peas to the hot pan and char them for about a minute on all sides. Transfer the snap peas to a mixing bowl and add the pea shoots, spring onion, celery leaves, and parsley.

Heat the olive oil in a small sauté pan over medium heat. Fry the anchovies lightly, stirring constantly, until they have crisped up and broken into shards. Turn off the heat and pour in the lemon juice, being careful to avoid the splattering oil. Pour the warm anchovy mixture into the mixing bowl with the snap pea salad and toss to combine.

To serve, spoon 2 tablespoons of parsley pistou into the center of each plate. Heap a mound of the warm snap pea salad on top and rest a chop on one side of the salad. Top each chop with some additional pistou.

BOEUF

BOURGUIGNON

"À LA MINUTE"

1½ pounds
BEEF TENDERLOIN,
cut into 1-inch cubes

FINE SEA SALT

BLACK PEPPER

8 ounces
BACON,
cut into ½-inch by 1-inch strips

16
PEARL ONIONS,
peeled

16
**SMALL, YOUNG
CARROTS,** *OR*
4 LARGE CARROTS,
quartered

2 tablespoons
UNSALTED BUTTER

4 cloves
GARLIC,
smashed

1 cup
MIXED MUSHROOMS,
cut to approximately the same
size as the beef cubes

½ cup
DRY RED WINE

3 tablespoons
**CHOPPED FRESH
FLAT-LEAF PARSLEY**

2 cups
BORDELAISE SAUCE
(page 6)

2 teaspoons
LEMON JUICE

Serves 4

The *boeuf* in this bourguignon is served medium-rare, a nice departure from the fall-apart texture of a usual braise—and a neat party trick, too. The stew's long-simmered, rich flavors and spoon-coating consistency are built in advance, thanks to our bordelaise sauce.

Season the beef generously with salt and pepper. In a medium Dutch oven, cook the bacon over medium heat until browned. Remove the bacon with a slotted spoon and set aside on paper towels to drain. Turn the heat up to high and sear the beef in the bacon fat, browning it quickly but leaving the inside as rare as possible. Set the beef aside and discard the fat from the pot.

Fill a medium saucepan with water and bring to a boil. Prepare an ice water bath. Blanch the onions and carrots, separately, until they're cooked through but still firm, and cool in the ice water. Set aside.

Melt 1 tablespoon of the butter in the same pot over medium heat and sauté the garlic, onions, and carrots. When the vegetables are lightly caramelized, add the mushrooms and cook until they have released all their moisture and caramelized a bit, about 10 minutes. Add the red wine, bring to a simmer, and reduce by half. Return the browned bacon and beef to the pot and add the parsley and bordelaise sauce. Bring the stew just to a boil and then remove it from the heat. Stir in the remaining 1 tablespoon of butter and the lemon juice. Add a pinch more salt, if needed, and divide equally among four bowls.

DINDE AU VIN

(TURKEY BRAISED IN RED WINE WITH PORK BELLY & MUSHROOMS)

4
LARGE TURKEY WINGS

FINE SEA SALT

CANOLA OIL

8 ounces
PORK BELLY,
at least 1 inch thick

20
PEARL ONIONS,
peeled

1 large
CARROT,
diced

1 cup
QUARTERED CREMINI MUSHROOMS

1 (750 ml) bottle
DRY RED WINE

2 cups
RUBY PORT

1 strip
ORANGE PEEL
(about 1 inch by 2 inches)

1
CINNAMON STICK

½ teaspoon
BLACK PEPPER

The turkey wing, a bit player on the Thanksgiving stage, gets a starring role in this variation on a traditional coq au vin. With each wing weighing in at almost a pound (although much of that is bone), a single wing is sufficient for a generous portion.

Preheat your oven to 400°F. Using a chef's knife, separate the turkey wings at the joint. Season the wing pieces liberally with salt and lay them in a single layer on a rimmed baking sheet. Brush the wings with canola oil and roast until they're golden brown, about 30 minutes.

Cut the pork belly into 1-inch cubes. Coat the bottom of a large, heavy-bottomed Dutch oven with canola oil and heat it over high heat. When the oil begins to smoke, add the pork cubes and brown them on all sides. Use a slotted spoon to transfer them to a plate lined with paper towels to drain. Lower the flame to medium and sauté the onions, carrot, and mushrooms in the pork fat, stirring frequently, until lightly caramelized, about 10 minutes. Add the red wine, port, orange peel, cinnamon stick, and pepper to the pot, bring the liquid to a simmer, and reduce it by about a quarter, about 10 minutes. Return the wings and pork to the pot and simmer until the turkey meat is tender, about 1 hour.

Divide the stew among four bowls and serve.

LAMB
CLUB
SANDWICH

1 (2-pound)
BONELESS LAMB LEG

**EXTRA-VIRGIN
OLIVE OIL**

FINE SEA SALT

8
**SALT-PACKED WHOLE
ANCHOVIES,**
rinsed and boned, *OR*
**16 OIL-PACKED
ANCHOVY FILLETS**

4 cloves
GARLIC,
peeled

1
LAMB BELLY
(aka lamb breast),
1 to 1¼ pounds

1 loaf
OLIVE BREAD

2 bunches
ARUGULA

1
LEMON

2 tablespoons
**CHOPPED FRESH
ROSEMARY**

½ cup
AIOLI
(page 4)

8
**OVEN-DRIED
TOMATOES**
(page 16)

We've never managed to find a place for this sandwich on our menus, but it's one of our favorites at home. And although it's intended to be served warm, this is one of those sandwiches that's a different kind of wonderful after it sits for a while—say, in a picnic basket. Once again, anchovies are doing their secret work of making things taste better.

Preheat your oven to 450°F. Place the lamb leg on a rack set in a roasting pan. Rub it all over with olive oil and season liberally with salt. Using a paring knife, make 16 shallow incisions all over the lamb. Cut the anchovy fillets in half (if using oil-packed fillets, leave them whole) and the garlic cloves into quarters and tuck a piece of each into the pockets. Roast the lamb for 25 minutes, then lower the oven temperature to 325°F and continue to cook for another 25 minutes, or until the internal temperature of the lamb reaches 125°F. Remove the pan from the oven and transfer the lamb to a cutting board to rest. Pour the pan drippings into a bowl. Turn the oven up to 400°F.

Rub the lamb belly with olive oil and salt and place it on the same rack in the roasting pan. Roast until brown and crispy, about 20 minutes. Pour the pan drippings into the same bowl with the drippings from the leg.

Cut 12 thick slices of olive bread. Brush the bread with olive oil and toast in a panini press, grill pan, or your oven. In a medium bowl, toss the arugula with a squeeze of lemon, a drizzle of olive oil, and salt to taste. In a small bowl, mix the rosemary into the aioli.

Cut the lamb belly into strips and slice the lamb leg thinly.

To assemble the sandwiches, spread the rosemary aioli on the toasted olive bread and make four double-decker sandwiches, dividing the warm sliced lamb, crispy lamb belly, oven-dried tomatoes, and arugula between the layers.

STEAK FRITES

There is no better piece of beef than a properly seared steak and no finer potato than a golden-brown french fry—and there may be no better meal on Earth than the two of them paired together in the quintessential French bistro dish: steak frites. The ingredients are simple. From that point on, it's all about technique and procedure. The recipe begins with a visit to your butcher.

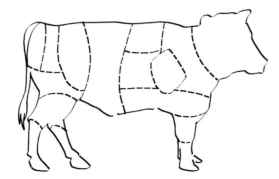

Shopping for a Steak

Beef definitely falls into the "you get what you pay for" category. Inexpensive beef is readily available, but cheap meat is gross: it's bad for the animals, for your body, and for the environment. Visit a local farmers' market or a butcher that sells meat from cattle that are raised on smaller farms and allowed to graze on carefully maintained grasses. If you're in Brooklyn, go to Fleishers in Park Slope or the Meat Hook in Williamsburg, both of which buy beautiful, whole animals from small farms. The meat you'll find there is more expensive than anything at a supermarket, but the quality will knock your socks off. It's a luxury item, not something you would have every day, which is probably for the best.

Selecting a Steak

You can make a great meal out of the humblest cut (often the choice for steak frites) or the fanciest dry-aged luxury steak. You can also completely screw up *any* steak. The journey to a delicious steak frites begins with choosing the right steak and knowing how to handle it properly.

Selecting your steak is a matter of what you're in the mood for as well as what you're willing to pay. In general, the more expensive cuts are from around the ribs and spine of the animal. These muscles are thick and well marbled and naturally tender because they don't do too much work. Such cuts remain juicy and tender even when cooked beyond medium (provided they are properly rested) and may be served without slicing to preserve their heat, and for the pleasure of tearing apart a steak with a sharp knife.

The inexpensive cuts come from all over the animal, often from muscles that are thinner and toughened by exercise. On the plus side, they can also be wonderfully flavorful. They benefit from being cooked quickly over high heat and from being served sliced, which makes for a more tender bite of meat and a nicer presentation (these cuts are generally less pretty when whole).

The following are a few of our favorites from both categories of steaks.

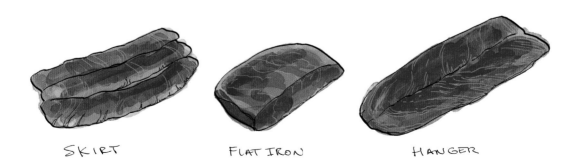

SKIRT   FLAT IRON   HANGER

CHEAP(ER) STEAKS

Skirt Steak: Rich and beefy, skirt steak is one of the thinner cuts, so it needs to be cooked quickly over high heat to get a nice crust on the exterior in the short time it takes to cook the interior. The best scenario for this steak is a super-hot charcoal grill. For the sake of presentation and tenderness, it is especially important to serve skirt steak thinly sliced against the grain.

Flatiron Steak: A favorite at our restaurants, the flatiron steak is almost as tender as tenderloin but with far more marbling. Flatiron steaks are also conveniently uniform in thickness and nicely rectangular, which makes them easy to cook and slice.

Hanger Steak: This thin, loose-grained steak is delicious but no good at all if overcooked. Like the skirt steak, hanger is best seared quickly on a hot grill and sliced against the grain.

LUXURY STEAKS

Rib Eye: When served bone-in, a rib eye is magnificent hunk of beef, highly marbled and tender, that will feed at least two people. They may also be removed from the bone and cut thinner to make single-serving steaks.

Strip Steak: The strip is less marbled than the rib eye and somewhat chewier, qualities that some find preferable. The size and shape of the steak make it easy to cook evenly and to negotiate with a steak knife.

Porterhouse: The porterhouse is kind of a compound steak, with its signature T-shaped bone dividing a piece of strip from a piece of tenderloin. Ask for a center cut, which will have a larger piece of tenderloin attached, and for a thickness of at least 2 inches.

A NOTE ON DRY-AGED BEEF

Dry-aged beef is beef that has been stored, unwrapped, in a cooler for as little as 2 weeks and as long as 60 days (even longer by some meat-aging freaks). During this time, the meat loses some of its moisture and becomes more tender and flavorful thanks to natural enzymatic and bacterial activity inside and on its surface. As aging progresses, the exterior of the beef transforms into a hard, dry crust while the usable portion of the meat becomes smaller (and increasingly expensive).

Preferences vary as to just how aged a steak ought to be. While a steak with 14 to 28 days of age would be a treat for just about any carnivore, dry-aging gets divisive when

RIBEYE

STRIP

you get to the longer end of the age spectrum. Beef that's aged longer than 30 days starts to get funky-tasting, and it keeps getting funkier the longer it ages. This quality has been described as beefy, nutty, and even "cheese-like." To some people, well-aged beef is one of the world's greatest delicacies; to others, it's kind of gross. If you're new to the world of dry-aged beef, start out on the lower end of the aging spectrum (14 days) and work your way up to the level that you prefer. It's an indulgence–dry-aged beef is at least twice as expensive as fresh beef–so you should dip your toe before you dive in.

Cooking a Steak

A steak dinner can be a stressful occasion. You're cooking one of the world's most expensive ingredients and everyone's counting on you to not screw it up. Your challenge: searing a crunchy, caramelized exterior in the time it takes the steak's interior to arrive at your ideal shade of red, pink, or beyond. Whether you're cooking outdoors over glowing hardwood coals or over the electric burner in your tiny apartment kitchen, these results are within reach.

THE BASICS

Preheat your pan or grill. There's really no such thing as too hot. Preheat a grill with the lid closed.

Season your steaks. A generous sprinkling of salt and cracked black pepper is an important component of your crunchy, caramelized crust. It takes more salt than you think. Don't worry, most of it is going to come off in the pan or fall through the grill. And remember, the interior of the steak isn't getting any salt at all.

Flip once, then flip again. This runs contrary to conventional steak wisdom, but it definitely makes a difference. The finished steak will be more evenly cooked on the inside.

Rest it. This is the most commonly overlooked step; sadly, it's also the one that makes all the difference. When you cut into a steak that isn't properly rested, its juices run all over the place, leaving a dry steak behind. People like their steaks cooked all different ways, but no one likes a dry steak. Steaks should rest for approximately half the time they spent cooking.

Slather it with butter while it rests. Plain butter is nice, but a compound butter like Maître d'Hôtel (page 163) will perfume your steak with herbs and garlic while it rests.

DETERMINING DONENESS

Our steak recipes list estimated cooking times for a 1-inch-thick medium-rare steak. The timing may be adjusted for thicker steaks or different degrees of doneness. If you'd like to skip the calculations and eliminate all uncertainty, you can use a thermometer. A digital internal probe thermometer will give you an accurate temperature in just a few seconds, a guarantee of what you'll see when you slice into that steak.

Whichever cooking method you use, the following are the internal temperatures you're looking for:

RARE 115°F
MEDIUM-RARE 125°F
MEDIUM 135°F
MEDIUM-WELL 150°F
WELL-DONE 160°F

Note: *If your steak is 1½ inches or thicker, remove it from the heat at an internal temperature that's 5 degrees below these targets, because the internal temperature will continue to increase significantly while it rests.*

COOKING METHODS

Cooking times are for a 1-inch-thick steak at medium-rare. For a thicker steak, increase the time in each step by 1 minute.

Gas or Charcoal Grill: Preheat your grill with the lid closed until it's as hot as it can get, and season it with a kitchen towel lightly coated with canola oil when you're ready to cook the steak. Put your seasoned steak on the grill and immediately close the lid again. Grill for 2 minutes, flip, and replace the lid. After 2 more minutes, flip again (rotating 90 degrees for nice-looking grill marks) and grill for 1 minute with the lid open. Flip one last time, and cook for 1 more minute. This will yield a steak that is medium-rare. For a medium to medium-well steak, increase the cooking time in each step by 1 minute. This method will vary slightly depending on your grill. When your steak is ready to come off the grill, slather with butter or Maître d'Hôtel butter (page 163), rest, and serve.

Cast-Iron Skillet: To minimize heat loss and avoid steaming your meat, use a pan large enough to leave plenty of room around the steaks. Cook them in batches if necessary.

Preheat the pan over high heat until it's smoking hot. Pour in ⅛ inch of canola oil and heat until it begins to smoke. Add your seasoned steak to the pan, pressing it down gently, and cook until well browned on the bottom, about 2 minutes. Flip and brown the second side for about 2 minutes. Flip the steak again and lower the heat to medium, then add 1 tablespoon of unsalted butter, along with a smashed clove of garlic and a sprig of thyme, if you like. Use a spoon to baste the top of the meat with the butter for 1 minute. Flip and baste the opposite side for 1 minute. Slather with more butter, or Maître d'Hôtel butter (page 163), rest, and serve.

COOKING
STEAKS FOR
A PARTY

*Cooking steaks for a large group in a home kitchen is
a messy affair. By the time you've got your steaks on the table, your
house is full of smoke and your guests have been deprived
of your sparkling wit for far too long.*

To give your house a while to air out and yourself the time to enjoy a drink,
you can cook your steaks an hour or more in advance and allow them to rest
at room temperature. Just before you're ready to serve, slather your steaks
with a compound or plain butter and heat them for 1½ to 2 minutes on the
top shelf of your oven under a well-preheated broiler. Alternatively, if you
grilled your steaks outside, keep the grill hot, then turn off one section of the
burners (or move the coals to one side) and reheat the buttered steaks for
1½ to 2 minutes on the cooler side.

Maître d'Hôtel Butter

Makes about 2½ cups

Compound butters are like the astronaut ice cream of sauces, melting on contact to bathe your steak with richness and herbaceous aromas. Maître d'Hôtel butter is the mother of them all, a combination that would improve just about any cooked thing.

4 sticks
UNSALTED BUTTER,
at room temperature

¼ cup
CHOPPED
FRESH TARRAGON

¼ cup
CHOPPED
FRESH FLAT-LEAF PARSLEY

¼ cup
CHOPPED
FRESH CHIVES

2
SHALLOTS,
minced

GRATED ZEST OF 1 LEMON

Put everything in a bowl and stir to combine. Store in an airtight container in the refrigerator for up to 2 weeks. Allow the butter to come to room temperature before using.

Pommes Frites (French Fries)

Serves 4

French fries must be hot, well salted, golden brown, crispy on the outside, and soft in the middle. Four out of five ain't frites. It takes time, care, and a lot of hot oil, but a great french fry is a beautiful thing.

4 large
RUSSET POTATOES

4 quarts
CANOLA OIL

FINE SEA SALT

Special Equipment

CANDY OR DEEP-FRY THERMOMETER

FRYER BASKET

Find a container that will be large enough to hold all your cut potatoes and fill it halfway with water. With a large, sharp knife, square off the sides and ends off each potato. Cut the potatoes into ¼-inch slices, then cut each slice into ¼-inch batons. As soon as you cut them, immediately drop the cut potatoes in the water, adding more water if needed to keep them submerged. For the crispiest fries, soak the cut potatoes in the refrigerator overnight; that's what we do at the restaurants. If you don't have a day to wait, they may be cooked immediately with good results.

FRY #1

In a large pot or Dutch oven, heat the canola oil until the temperature reaches 325°F on a candy thermometer. Drain the cut potatoes in a colander, then return them to the soaking container and refill with fresh water. Drain the potatoes a second time, submerge in fresh water again, and hold for frying.

When the oil is up to temperature, fill the fryer basket halfway with potatoes and shake well (away from your pot of hot oil) to throw off any excess water. Carefully lower the basket into the hot oil. Fry for 6 minutes, gently shaking the basket once every minute so the fries don't stick together and the oil is able to circulate evenly around them.

Lift the basket from the oil and carefully remove one fry to test. A properly parcooked french fry should still be as pale as raw potato and should be soft enough to just collapse between your fingers when squeezed, without breaking apart. If the fries need more cooking time, return them to the oil for another minute or two. When they're finished cooking, turn the fries out onto a baking sheet in a single layer to cool. Repeat this process until all the potatoes are parcooked.

FRY #2

Bring the temperature of the oil up to 360°F. Fill the fryer basket halfway with parcooked fries and gently lower it into the hot oil. Shaking frequently, fry until they are golden brown and crispy, about 4 minutes. Turn the cooked fries out onto a baking sheet lined with paper towels and season generously with salt. Repeat with the remaining potatoes. Serve immediately.

Note: *An electric deep-fryer may be used for this recipe, following the manufacturer's instructions on how much oil to use.*

Pommes Frites

SETTING THE STAGE

A dining room's job is to serve up the romance, coaxing you out of everyday life into a place where your only job is to relax and enjoy. When we built Buttermilk Channel, our budget didn't afford us the luxury of an architect, designer, or even a real contractor. This was both a curse and a blessing. A little expertise would have saved us a few hundred hours of frustration, but being on our own forced us to consider an important question: What makes certain restaurants feel so magical?

We hit the town, determined to unearth some secrets. Armed with measuring tapes and cell phone cameras, we surreptitiously surveyed some of New York's best dining rooms, relaying dimensions and inspirations back to our construction site.

How far from the surface of the bar should a pendant hang, so that you can see your food and a book without feeling like you're being interrogated? How many inches should the bar protrude, so you can comfortably eat a meal without smashing your knees–or spilling on them? How wide does a communal table need to be to accommodate your food without forcing you to shout at your date across its vast expanse? (That would be thirty inches; thank you, Keith McNally.) Which shade of creamy yellow paint will make the room glow?

It's our job to throw two dinner parties a day, but we still enjoy the busman's holiday of entertaining at home. And a lot of what we learned in the process of building Buttermilk Channel (and later, from working on French Louie with our genius designer, Joseph Foglia) has helped us make our own dinner parties at home a little nicer.

Lights. Use your dimmers. A too-dark party is better than one that's too bright. Plug-in lamp dimmers are available at any hardware store (and will come in handy if you like to read in bed even though your spouse goes to bed three hours before you get home).

An evenly lit room feels dull; use dimmers and plenty of candles (see below) to create pools of shade and light. Ideally, there will be many light sources, some up high, some lower.

Party lighting should be warm, which means incandescent lightbulbs. Turn off halogen and fluorescent overheads and rely on candles and spot lighting instead.

Candles. Candles make light come to life—they twinkle and dance and move. Not to mention that they actually warm you—which is why we put out way fewer of them in the hottest days of August.

As far as your own party goes, candles are cheap, they'll make your house look fancy, and their light makes everyone look great. Don't skimp: having lots of them is transformative.

Temperature. The temperature of the room is a matter of preparation. When it's freezing outside, people want to enter to a warm blast. When it's scorching out, we pre-chill the room aggressively before we open, eating family meal in scarves, so it has a fighting chance of staying cold when the door opens. If you've ever wondered why your ordinarily comfortable apartment is suddenly sweltering during a party, it's because *people are hot.*

At the extremes, there's only so much a thermostat can do. If your AC has reached its limit, make sure to have plenty of cold beer and lemonade on hand—or warm your chilly guests from the inside by greeting them with hot toddies, cider, or coffee.

Music. It's always powerful to see how quickly the mood of the room changes when the music does. The right soundtrack can inject energy into a flagging room, or chill everybody right out.

We've learned to go with the flow: the cool side of bebop, all brushy drums and tinkly piano, can make a near-empty dining room feel like the place to be, but it'll get lost once the room fills with voices. When the restaurant starts to fill, we give people music to dance to (and we know we've gotten it right when people are singing along in their seats). Anything goes at the peak of the evening or during a busy brunch, just as long as the energy is high. Later, as people relax over one last after-dinner drink, it's time for something a little sexier, more laid back.

We've found that new music never works as well as the oldies (even if the good old days were just two years ago). A generous dose of nostalgia helps. It's fun to watch as a favorite song envelops a group of friends in a haze of happy memories, and we often see music bring strangers together, too: Who is this again? You remember where you were when this song came out?

At all hours, we like our music a little bit loud (sorry, Dad). Just as with salt, if no one's complaining, it's probably time to turn it up a notch.

WINE

EVERY TUESDAY NIGHT at Buttermilk Channel, we invite
our customers to bring their own wines to dinner. The bottles people show up
with span the entire spectrum, from the ten-dollar bargain bin find to the most
expensive and rare old wines on Earth. This table is drinking Grand Cru
Burgundy, that one a simple Beaujolais, and the couple in the
corner's got a novelty rosé with a naughty label left over from a bridal shower.
These wines are as different as can be, but the plates that sit next to them,
more often than not, hold the same thing: fried chicken and cheddar waffles. The
moral of this story is twofold. First: fried chicken is really good with wine.
Second: you don't need to pull your hair out figuring out what to drink with
dinner. Usually, the best wine to drink is the wine you like best.

Talking Wine

You read menus with your imagination, using experience and appetite to put together a meal. Wine lists can be a little harder—unless you're already familiar with the region, vintage, and producer, you may be in for an unhappy surprise. We love to talk about wine, and we want to bring you the bottle that will make your heart sing. In order to get there, it helps to have a common language.

Light-, medium-, full-bodied: These terms are relative, of course; but a fairly objective measure of the body of a wine is its percentage of alcohol by volume. Wines in the lower range, 11 to 13 percent, will feel lighter than wines at higher levels.

Acidity: All good wines have some discernible acidity. In the absence of acidity, wine tastes flat. Some wines are more acidic than others, and this is a good thing to identify and request. There's one good, old-fashioned rule of wine pairing that says that high-acid wines are good with foods that you would put lemon juice on, such as fish, shellfish, or salads.

Tannin: Tannins are naturally occurring polyphenols that come mainly from grape skins and stems and are, therefore, found in red wines. (Reds get their color from leaving the grape skins in the tank during fermentation.) Tannins create a drying sensation on your tongue that can be pleasant or harsh depending on your preferences and what foods you are drinking it with. Too much tannin—sometimes a problem with big red wines drunk too young—is never a good thing. A moderate level will go nicely with rich and meaty foods, though, so if you have a steak or roast chicken in your future, you may want to request a red with some structure.

If you're feeling adventurous or trusting, you can describe your wine preferences using these terms alone and see what you get served. You may wind up with an old favorite or something unfamiliar, but it will probably be a wine you like. To drill down further, consider which of the following qualities you're looking for.

Fruit: Saying that you do or do not want a fruity wine is helpful, but most wine tastes like at least one kind of fruit, so you may need to be more specific. Most white wine has some lemony or other citrus flavor. If that's completely absent, then that wine is probably the kind we call "flabby," lacking in the acidity that makes a wine appealing.

Whites made from certain grapes under certain conditions taste of stone fruits—think: apricots, peaches, and so on.

We like to describe red wines on a cherry scale that goes like this: tart cherry → ripe cherry → overripe cherry → cooked cherry. Wines on all parts of this scale can be delicious, provided that these fruit notes are in balance with other qualities.

Earth, minerality: Earthiness is a gorgeous quality found in some of the best wines in the world. When we describe a wine as earthy, we mean that it has certain aromas that are not reminiscent of fruit and that may bring to mind the taste of mushrooms, or the smell of a clump of moist soil or of a wet stone. Earthiness is a characteristic we associate more with red wines, although there are some wonderful white exceptions. Great Chablis, for example, develop beautiful mushroomy aromas after about 10 years of age.

Minerality is a flavor or aroma that evokes inorganic substances like clay, salt, and stones. Taste that same Chablis when it's young and you'll know what minerality means.

What (Not) to Drink

We're not big fans of "pairing," the supposed art of matching the correct wine with each dish. The wine pairers of the world have the best intentions, but their school of thought creates unnecessary stress about making a mistake. Rather than memorizing a dubious list of what goes with what, you might be better off turning this pairing idea on its head and remembering the few truly disgusting food and wine combinations that you should definitely avoid.

FOOD & WINE
COMBINATIONS TO AVOID

Tannic reds with spicy foods

Tannins react with hot spices or heat from peppers to make your hearty Cabernet taste really bitter. Fish oils have a nasty reaction with tannins, too.

High-acid foods with low-acid wines

When you're eating raw oysters, for example, your wine needs to be pretty tart, otherwise it will taste flat and flabby.

Sweet foods with dry wines

Sweets will bring out some unappealing, often bitter, notes in those wines.

Stinky cheeses with just about any wine

At best your wine will be overpowered; at worst you may experience some uniquely gross flavors. Beers and ciders, on the other hand, tend to be excellent with cheese. We have some strong feelings about this (see page 174).

That's about it. A light, tart, minerally white wine might not be what everyone would want with a big, fat steak, but if light, tart, minerally whites make you happier than any red wine does, then that's what you should have. Cheers!

CHEESE

slab *n* \ *slab* \ [ME slabbe] 1. A thick plate or slice.
2. (Brooklyn, 2008) A portion of cheese large enough to
enjoy and share without inciting envy or hostility.

When we opened Buttermilk Channel in 2008, we scoured the neighborhood for local ingredients to use in our kitchen. Carroll Gardens, home to a large Italian community that eats very well, did not disappoint. We only had to head down Court Street to find fiery hot sausages at Esposito's Pork Store and fresh linguine and ethereal mozzarella at Caputo's Fine Foods.

Another neighbor, Anne Saxelby, had recently opened a tiny cheese shop in the Essex Street Market on the Lower East Side. There are a number of excellent cheese purveyors in this city, but Anne's shop—though much smaller than the competition—was different in one, groundbreaking way: it sold only American cheeses, most of them from not very far away and all of them the kind of gutsy, nuanced, handmade gems you'd find in a market in France or Italy.

We didn't even have to cross the bridge; Anne would bike by on her way home from work, her magical basket loaded with great stinking wedges. Anne's bicycle has been upgraded to a delivery truck, but our three-times-a-week order has never changed: bring us whatever you love.

Putting Together a Selection

Cheese doesn't need to be limited to the cocktail party buffet or a course at the end of a meal. One or two nice cheeses alongside a bowl of soup and a salad makes a lovely, quick dinner.

If cheese is the main event, you'll need at least three. Our menus always offer one that's soft and rich, one that's blue, and one that's either crumbly and nutty or semi-firm and sweet. Either the blue or the soft cheese will be stinky, but probably not both. Pay attention

SERVING
CHEESE

Whether you're serving a single, perfect wedge or putting out a 12-foot-long plateau de fromages extraordinaires (with 48 hours' notice, we can do that for you), here are a few guidelines for bringing out the best in your cheese.

There should be lots of it.

Order cheese at our restaurants, and we'll clobber you with fat slabs of the stuff. We use that term—slab—both on our menus and in our kitchens so we won't forget to give you enough.

Take it out of the fridge at least an hour before serving.

Cheese is aromatic, sometimes alarmingly so, and cold is an aroma-killer. Cold cheese has texture problems, too. Serve yours at room temperature.

Accompaniments should provide a nice contrast, but not overwhelm the star of the show.

Salty and pungent cheeses are good with sweet things (preserves, dried fruits), while soft cheeses are good with crunchy things (nuts, toasts, crackers). Most cheeses are good with sour things, like our Vinegar Roasted Grapes (page 175), and pungent, stinky cheeses are complemented by something sweet, like our Black Pepper Fig Conserve (page 22).

to balancing the salt levels in your selection or you'll be thirsty for days.

Most shops sell cheeses from all over the world, but why not narrow your selection to one country or, better yet, a single region within? Like serving the wine of a country alongside its cuisine, it feels appropriate, and the resulting selection tends to work together coherently.

What to Drink with Cheese

We're not trying to start any trouble here, but why do we automatically pair wine with cheese?

They're like a bad couple, always fighting and rarely complementing each other. Wines clash with pungent, stinky cheeses the way they do with spicy and sweet foods. Even when they don't clash, cheese often overpowers a wine.

Let's not fight with each other or our cheeses—how about some hard cider and beer instead? Really stinky cheeses need sweetness, which most ciders and beers have in varying degrees, and the cool temperature and bubbles in these drinks provide a refreshing contrast.

Cheese is peanut butter; cider is jelly. There's no room for wine in that sandwich.

Our Favorites

It is hard to name our favorite cheeses—there are too many—but here are a few we especially love, all of which are available (seasonally) from Saxelby Cheesemongers (SaxelbyCheese.com):

Queso del Invierno from Vermont Shepherd (Westminster, Vermont): This is a firm, nutty "winter cheese," which means it's been aged for several cold months. It's also highly addictive and induces feelings of euphoria (in us, anyway).

Cabot Clothbound Cheddar from Cabot Creamery (Cabot, Vermont) and the Cellars at Jasper Hill Farm (Greensboro Bend, Vermont): This collaboration between the cheddar behemoth and Jasper Hill, a small, artisanal cheesemaker, is Cabot Creamery's best expression of its love for cheddar. It's a beautifully aged cheese that's firm and rich with a hint of nutty-sweet caramel. It's also great for grating (cheese pun, please forgive us).

Red Rock Cheese from Roelli Cheese Haus (Shullsburg, Wisconsin): As Uncle Mike would say, this blue-veined orange cheddar offers a "little bit of BOB," or best of both. It's aged to perfection—a little salty and a little sharp, with a slight crumble—making it outstanding on a cheese board and mind-blowing on a burger.

Cayuga Blue from Lively Run Goat Dairy (Interlaken, New York): This blue cheese is made entirely from goat's milk. It's sweet and creamy, with a firm texture and veins of salty blue mold.

Oma from the von Trapp Farmstead (Waitsfield, Vermont) and the Cellars at Jasper Hill Farm (Greensboro Bend, Vermont): Yes, those von Trapps! They made it over the mountain and settled in Vermont, where they produce this lovely cheese. With your first bite you will be instantly transformed into an Austrian child with an amazing knack for harmony. Pungent, salty, and a little bit funky, this cheese is creamy and spreadable at room temperature.

Hooligan from Cato Corner Farm (Colchester, Connecticut): This washed-rind cheese really stinks, which is a good thing when you're talking about cheeses. Set this one in a corner of the room at the beginning of your dinner party and let it slowly come up to room temperature. When the smell permeates the room and conversation comes to an uncomfortable silence, it's ready to be devoured.

Vinegar Roasted Grapes

2 pounds black seedless grapes
1 cup balsamic vinegar

Preheat your oven to 450°F. Spread the grapes out in a single layer on a rimmed baking sheet or a full-size hotel pan. Pour the balsamic vinegar over the grapes.

Place the pan in the oven and cook until the grapes just start to pop, about 10 minutes. Remove them from the oven and let cool in the pan. Transfer the grapes and any remaining liquid to a container with a tight-fitting lid. Pickled grapes will hold for up to a week, refrigerated.

Recipes
FOR

FRENCH TOAST PANCAKES CRÊPES

SCRAMBLES BISCUITS GRITS

BRUNCH

20 FOUNDATIONAL RECIPES

EVERYONE'S STARVING BY the time they get to the first meal of the day. So, while our brunch food is designed for comfort, the recipes are built for speed. Most of the dishes in this chapter can be prepped at least a day in advance, meaning that you can enjoy the party the night before and still get food on the table for your houseguests before things get ugly. When applicable, these recipes contain a note suggesting the steps that you can get out of the way to make your morning cooking a breeze, even if your head is still in a fog.

PECAN PIE FRENCH TOAST 182

PANCAKES 184

CHICKPEA SOCCA
& SUNNY-SIDE UP EGGS
WITH MIXED GRAINS & CAULIFLOWER 187

BUCKWHEAT CRÊPES
WITH RICOTTA & APPLE BUTTER 190

EGGS BENEDICT
EGGS HUNTINGTON 194
EGGS LOUIE 195

CURED STEELHEAD TROUT
WITH HASH BROWNS & LEMON-CAPER
CRÈME FRAÎCHE 196

"LEFTOVERS" FRITTATA 199

CORPSE REVIVER NO. 2
THE FANCIEST BRUNCH COCKTAIL OF THEM ALL 216

IN PRAISE OF THE SCRAMBLE
MUSHROOM & GOAT CHEESE SCRAMBLE 200
CURED STEELHEAD TROUT SCRAMBLE 201
PIPÉRADE & MERGUEZ SCRAMBLE 201

A-B-C GRILLED CHEESE 202

GRAPEFRUIT & ENDIVE SALAD 203

CORDON BLEU 204

BREAKFAST SAUSAGE 207

BUTTERMILK BISCUITS 208

GRITS 210

SHORT RIB HASH 211

BLOODY MARY:
THE DRINK THAT EATS LIKE A MEAL 212

KINDNESS AND
SALT
WITH THE SUN OUT

Brunch reveals another side of our restaurants, an alternative personality that emerges on Saturday and Sunday mornings. On weekends from ten in the morning until three in the afternoon, our restaurants don't just serve brunch, they *become* brunch.

Dinner is a time for candlelight and cocktails, for relaxed three-course meals shared between friends and neighbors, families, and dates. At brunch, the cast is the same but their roles have changed. Bartenders put aside their nighttime repertoire of cocktails and beers to sling lattes, Bloody Marys, and mimosas. Some customers have been up with their kids since dawn and some are already back from a run, while bleary-eyed late risers stagger in with bedhead. Waiters dart about with daytime efficiency. There's no time for chitchat–these folks need coffee, fast.

Brunch brings all generations to the table. Hair-of-the-dog-swilling twentysomethings share communal tables with parents, grandparents, and babies. For once, kids and grown-ups can all agree on what to eat–it's French toast, pancakes, fried pork chops, and eggs any style all around.

As morning becomes afternoon and the kids leave for the playground, the coffee machine gets a rest, the drinks get stronger, and the music gets louder. Whitney Houston comes on the stereo and suddenly everyone is dancing. What's gotten into these people?

Brunch is a time of decadent fun and abundance, when everyone wants to go a little crazy, and everyone gets to have more–more food, more booze. Everything's sweeter, saltier, bigger, a little louder. The recipes you'll find in this chapter aren't your virtuous Monday-to-Friday avocado toasts; these are feasts for birthday breakfasts, holiday mornings, or a send-off after the wedding–one last hurrah before everyone goes home.

PECAN PIE
FRENCH TOAST

For the French Toast

2
BRIOCHE LOAVES,
about 12 inches long, unsliced

2 cups
WHOLE MILK

1 cup
HEAVY CREAM

2
LARGE EGGS, plus
2 LARGE EGG YOLKS

1 teaspoon
VANILLA EXTRACT

¼ cup
GRANULATED SUGAR

For the Pecan Sauce

8 tablespoons (1 stick)
UNSALTED BUTTER,
melted

¾ cup
CORN SYRUP

¼ cup
MOLASSES

3
LARGE EGGS

1 teaspoon
VANILLA EXTRACT

Shot of
BOURBON

1 cup
GRANULATED SUGAR

¼ teaspoon
FINE SEA SALT

1½ cups
CHOPPED PECANS

To Serve

UNSALTED BUTTER,
for griddling

CONFECTIONERS'
SUGAR,
for garnish (optional)

WHIPPED CREAM,
for garnish (optional)

Serves 8

The French *pain perdu*—literally "lost bread," or yesterday's stale bread dunked in eggs and milk and cooked for breakfast—provided the inspiration for this diner staple, and endless variations. Our distinctly American version at Buttermilk Channel swaps out the traditional maple syrup for the filling of a Southern pecan pie. The toast is cooked most of the way through in the oven, which makes it easy to prepare in advance when cooking for a crowd. You can complete the final steps just before serving. Brioche comes in all shapes and sizes, so you may need to improvise based on what you find at the bakery. Pyramidical wedges make a striking presentation, but if your loaf does not divide neatly into that shape, the results will be no less delicious.

Preheat your oven to 350°F and line a rimmed baking sheet with parchment paper.

To make the French toast, cut the loaves of brioche in half lengthwise, then cut pie-shaped wedges from each half. In a small bowl, combine the rest of the French toast ingredients in a bowl and whisk together until smooth. Transfer to a shallow baking dish that can hold the bread in a single layer without much extra space. Submerge the wedges in the batter and let them soak for about 10 minutes, flipping once so the bread gets completely saturated. Put the soaked bread on the lined baking sheet and bake for about 10 minutes, until golden brown. Remove and let cool.

To make the pecan sauce, whisk together all the ingredients in a small metal bowl set over a saucepan of simmering water. Cook, stirring occasionally, until the mixture is hot and has thickened to the consistency of honey. Hold the sauce at room temperature.

To serve, heat a large griddle or sauté pan over medium heat and melt enough butter to coat the surface of the pan. Working in batches, lightly brown the toast wedges on each side. Transfer the French toast to individual plates or a serving platter and top with the warm pecan sauce. If desired, dust the toast with confectioners' sugar and top with a dollop of whipped cream.

The Night Before: *Measure out the ingredients for the pecan sauce and store, covered, in the refrigerator. Cut the brioche into wedges and store, covered, at room temperature.*

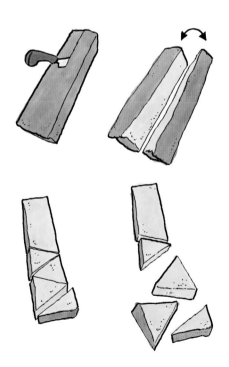

PANCAKES

3 cups
ALL-PURPOSE FLOUR

⅓ cup
SUGAR

2 tablespoons
BAKING POWDER

1 teaspoon
FINE SEA SALT

3
LARGE EGGS

1½ cups
BUTTERMILK

1 cup
WHOLE MILK

1 teaspoon
VANILLA EXTRACT

3 tablespoons
UNSALTED BUTTER,
melted

NONSTICK
COOKING SPRAY

MAPLE SYRUP,
for serving (optional)

SALTED BUTTER,
at room temperature, for
serving (optional)

Recipe Continues

Makes about 10 (6-inch) pancakes

A recipe for the ideal pancake (tender, fluffy, golden brown, barely sweet) will get you only halfway there—making them still takes some practice. Learning when to stop mixing, when the pan is ready for the batter, how to drop the batter to get a round shape, when to flip, and when to remove the pancake from the pan might take a few tries. But, once you've mastered it, you can spoil everyone on your vacation by waking up a little early to get these started.

Measure the flour, sugar, baking powder, and salt into a mixing bowl and whisk to combine. In a separate bowl, whisk together the eggs, buttermilk, milk, and vanilla until smooth. Add the wet ingredients to the dry ingredients and whisk together gently. When the batter is still a bit lumpy, stir in the melted butter with a few strokes of the whisk, then let the batter sit for 10 minutes at room temperature while the baking powder activates and the remaining lumps dissolve (see note #1).

Lightly grease a griddle or sauté pan with cooking spray and preheat over medium-high heat (see note #2). Test the cooking surface with a dime-size amount of pancake batter. If the bottom cooks in a few seconds, then you're ready to make pancakes.

Ladle out approximately ¼ cup of batter per pancake. The pancakes are ready to flip when small bubbles start to form on the top surface. Flip the pancakes and continue cooking until they're firm to the touch and golden on both sides.

Stack the pancakes into a giant tower à la Shel Silverstein. Serve "good little Grace" the one on top and save the middle pancake for "terrible Theresa." Top with maple syrup and butter.

Note #1: *You're trying to bring these ingredients together as gently as possible to avoid overworking the batter and ending up with pancakes that are tough or chewy rather than soft and tender.*

Note #2: *You can use butter or canola oil to cook the pancakes, but nonstick cooking spray will give you the easiest and most consistent results.*

The Night Before: *Whisk together the dry ingredients and store in a covered bowl or freezer bag.*

CHICKPEA SOCCA

& SUNNY-SIDE UP EGGS

with Mixed Grains & Cauliflower

◆

For the Socca

1 cup
CHICKPEA FLOUR

1 teaspoon
FINE SEA SALT

⅓ teaspoon
GROUND CUMIN

1¼ cups
WATER

1½ tablespoons
EXTRA-VIRGIN
OLIVE OIL

CANOLA OIL,
for cooking

For the Toppings

CANOLA OIL,
for cooking

1 medium head
CAULIFLOWER,
cut into small florets

1 cup
COOKED MIXED
GRAINS
(such as quinoa or farro)

COARSE SEA SALT

BLACK PEPPER

12
LARGE EGGS

¼ cup
CHOPPED
FRESH FLAT-LEAF
PARSLEY

EXTRA-VIRGIN
OLIVE OIL,
for drizzling

Recipe Continues

Socca

egg

grains

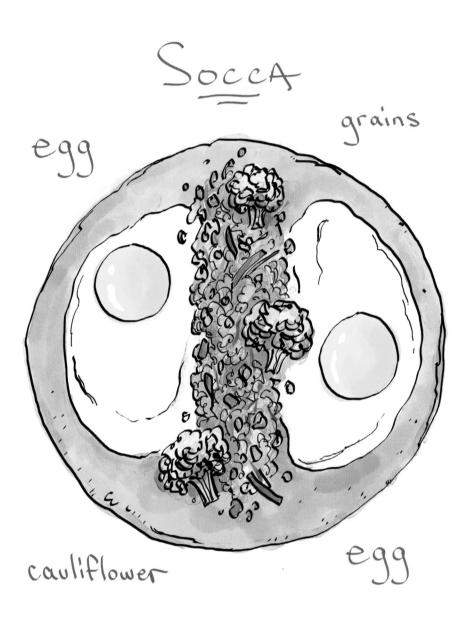

cauliflower

egg

Socca is a crispy chickpea crêpe native to Nice, on the Mediterranean coast of Provence. Niçoise street vendors roast their socca in wood-fired ovens, chop them into hot, fragrant shards, and serve them with a drizzle of olive oil, a sprinkle of sea salt, and a tumbler of icy rosé.

We like to use socca as the base for a dish—eggs, in this case. This crêpe is also an excellent gluten-free alternative to toasts or crackers to serve with hors d'oeuvres and dips.

To make the socca, combine the flour, salt, cumin, and water in a medium bowl and whisk until smooth. Whisk in the olive oil. Cover the batter and refrigerate for at least 2 hours or overnight. Remove the batter from the refrigerator 1 hour before cooking.

Preheat your broiler. Heat a medium cast-iron pan over high heat. Add enough canola oil to coat the pan and heat until smoking. Pour in enough socca batter to thinly coat the surface of the pan. When the edges begin to brown, transfer the pan to the broiler. When the top of the socca looks cooked and starts to blister, remove it from the pan to cool. Repeat with the remainder of the batter, stacking the cooked crêpes on a plate. If you're not using the batter all at once, it will keep in an airtight container in the refrigerator for up to 2 days.

To make the socca toppings, heat a medium sauté pan over medium heat, and add canola oil to coat the surface. Sauté the cauliflower florets until lightly caramelized. Add the cooked grains to the pan to warm them up. Season with salt and pepper to taste.

On a lightly greased griddle or another sauté pan, cook the eggs sunny-side up. The whites should be completely cooked and lightly brown on the edges, with a golden runny yolk. If you prefer your eggs poached, or scrambled, or over easy, that works, too.

To serve, top each socca with 2 eggs and spoon some cauliflower and grain mixture around them. Sprinkle with salt and parsley, and add a drizzle of olive oil.

The Night Before: *In addition to making the socca batter ahead of time, you can cut and sauté the cauliflower and allow it to cool, then store in a covered container in the refrigerator.*

BUCKWHEAT
CRÊPES

with Ricotta & Apple Butter

¾ cup
**ALL-PURPOSE
FLOUR**

½ cup
**BUCKWHEAT
FLOUR**

1 tablespoon
SUGAR

¼ teaspoon
FINE SEA SALT

2 cups
WHOLE MILK

3
LARGE EGGS

5 tablespoons
UNSALTED BUTTER,
melted

**NONSTICK COOKING
SPRAY**

2 cups
BUTTERMILK RICOTTA
(page 14)

1 cup
APPLE BUTTER
(page 20)

This dish strikes a nice balance between the sweet and savory ends of the brunch spectrum. Buckwheat flour has a minerally, nutty flavor, which makes a crêpe that's more than just a wrapper for your fillings. These crêpes are also great for a group because you can cook and fill them a day or more in advance, then heat them up in the oven before serving. Making crêpes takes a little practice, but the ingredients are inexpensive, and this recipe is sized to allow for a few failed attempts.

Measure the flours, sugar, and salt into a mixing bowl and whisk to combine. In a small bowl, beat together the milk and eggs. Add the wet ingredients to the dry ingredients and mix to combine completely. Slowly stir in the melted butter. Cover and refrigerate for at least 2 hours or as long as 24 hours before cooking.

Remove the batter from the refrigerator 30 minutes before cooking to allow it to come up a bit in temperature. Give it another stir before you cook it. Coat a medium nonstick pan with cooking spray and set it over high heat. When the pan starts to smoke, ladle about ¼ cup of batter into the center. Tilt and turn the pan to evenly distribute the batter. Cook for about a minute, until the underside is golden brown and releases easily from the pan, and flip with a spatula. Cook for about 10 seconds on the second side. Slide the crêpe onto a plate to cool. Repeat with the remaining batter, stacking the cooked crêpes on the plate.

Preheat your oven to 350°F and butter a rimmed baking sheet. Spoon about 2 tablespoons of ricotta in the center of each crêpe, then spread it evenly to about ½ inch from the edge. Fold each crêpe into a half circle, then in half again to make a triangle. Place the crêpes in a single layer on the prepared baking sheet.

Bake the crêpes for about 10 minutes, until they're warmed through and the edges begin to crisp. The apple butter may be warmed at this point or served at room temperature. Serve two or three crêpes per person, with a dollop of apple butter on top or on the side.

The Night Before: *Not only can the batter be made a day in advance, but the crêpes themselves can be made the night before, cooled, stacked on a plate, covered, and stored at room temperature. Or, if you have the refrigerator space, you can even fill and fold the crêpes, arrange them on the buttered baking sheet, cover, and store in the refrigerator. The cold crêpes will take a bit longer than 10 minutes to warm through.*

EGGS
BENEDICT

Two Variations

Eggs Benedict is a native New Yorker with a French pedigree. Conflicting histories trace its origins to either Delmonico's or the Waldorf—both the kind of gilded New York dining rooms where an all-American plate of ham and eggs might meet a fancy French sauce like hollandaise.

Just about any meat, fish, or vegetable is better with hollandaise sauce and poached eggs on it, so this dish has inspired many variations. Here are two of ours.

Note: All the components of eggs Benedict are warm, but they cool quickly. The steps of these recipes are written in the order that will get the dish to the table still steaming. Take a few minutes to get all your equipment and ingredients neatly laid out before you begin so nothing will get cold while you're rooting around in the pantry.

Eggs Huntington

Serves 4

Buttermilk Channel's entrance is on Court Street, but the kitchen door is on Huntington. It's a modest street with a fancy name of uncertain origins. A Huntington family? A place to hunt? On our side of that kitchen door, Huntington means this: poached eggs on a biscuit with salty ham and hollandaise. Don't be stingy with the hollandaise.

½ cup
DISTILLED WHITE VINEGAR

4
BUTTERMILK BISCUITS
(page 208)

8 thin slices
AMERICAN COUNTRY HAM
OR PROSCIUTTO

8
LARGE EGGS

1½ cups
HOLLANDAISE SAUCE
(page 8), kept warm

2 tablespoons
CHOPPED SCALLION

Preheat your broiler to toast the biscuits.

In a medium saucepan, bring about 2 quarts of water to a boil. Add the vinegar and reduce the heat to a simmer.

Split the biscuits in half and toast them lightly under the broiler. Put each biscuit on a plate, then top each half with a slice of ham.

Just before dropping the eggs into the simmering water, give it a swift stir with a slotted spoon. The momentum of the water will keep the egg whites compact. Crack the eggs into the swirling water and, after a minute, give the water another, gentler, stir. Poach the eggs for 3½ to 4 minutes, then remove them from the water with the slotted spoon and drain them on a plate lined with a clean kitchen towel.

To serve, gently place an egg on top of each half biscuit. Spoon a generous amount of warm hollandaise sauce over each egg. Top with chopped scallion and serve immediately.

The Night Before: *Bake the biscuits, allow them to cool, and store them in a covered container at room temperature.*

Eggs Louie

Serves 4

This is the Benedict we serve at Louie, all Frenched up with *sauce béarnaise*, crabmeat, and croissants in place of biscuits. Day-old croissants work well for this dish; they're easier to slice and they come back to life when you toast them.

**½ cup
DISTILLED WHITE VINEGAR**

**2
CROISSANTS**

**2 tablespoons
UNSALTED BUTTER**

**8 ounces
LUMP CRABMEAT**

**8
LARGE EGGS**

**1½ cups
BÉARNAISE SAUCE
(page 9), kept warm**

**2 tablespoons
CHOPPED SCALLION**

Preheat your broiler to toast the croissants.

In a medium saucepan, bring about 2 quarts of water to a boil. Add the vinegar and reduce the heat to a simmer.

Split the croissants in half from top to bottom, and then in half again crosswise. Toast the croissants under the broiler, then divide them among four plates.

Melt the butter in a small saucepan and add the crabmeat to gently warm it. Remove the pan from the heat and set aside.

Just before dropping the eggs into the simmering water, give it a swift stir with a slotted spoon. The momentum of the water will keep the egg whites compact. Crack the eggs into the swirling water and, after a minute, give the water another, gentler, stir. Poach the eggs for 3½ to 4 minutes, then lift them from the water with the slotted spoon and drain them on a plate lined with a clean kitchen towel.

To serve, place a spoonful of warm crab on each piece of croissant and top each with a poached egg. Douse each egg with a generous spoonful of béarnaise sauce. Top with chopped scallion and serve immediately.

The Night Before: *Make the reduction for the béarnaise sauce, cool, and hold in a covered container in the refrigerator.*

CURED
STEELHEAD TROUT

WITH HASH BROWNS & LEMON-CAPER CRÈME FRAÎCHE

For the Trout

1½ pounds skin-on center-cut
STEELHEAD TROUT FILLETS

1 cup
FINE SEA SALT

¾ cup
SUGAR

1 bunch
TARRAGON

2 tablespoons
GIN

3 tablespoons
BLACK PEPPER

For the Lemon-Caper Crème Fraîche

1 cup
CRÈME FRAÎCHE

GRATED ZEST AND JUICE OF 1 LEMON

2 tablespoons
CHOPPED CAPERS

1 teaspoon
POPPY SEEDS

For the Hash Browns

4
LARGE RUSSET POTATOES

1
LARGE EGG

¼ cup
finely chopped
SCALLIONS

CANOLA OIL,
for frying

FINE SEA SALT

Farm-raised steelhead trout is much closer to the quality of wild fish than farm-raised salmon; it's also considered to be a far more sustainable fish. That said, if steelhead isn't available for this recipe, wild or farm-raised salmon will work just fine. Ask your fishmonger for a center cut of the fish with the skin left intact. The cure takes a few days, but it's worth the wait.

Remove the pin bones from the trout using fish tweezers or your fingers.

Mix the salt and sugar in a small bowl. Spread out a third of the salt mixture in a shallow baking dish large enough to hold the trout, and put a few sprigs of tarragon on top. Lay the fish on the salt, skin side down. Drizzle the gin over the flesh of the fish and spread it around with your fingers to coat the surface. Sprinkle the pepper evenly to season. Top the fish with the rest of the tarragon and cover completely with the remaining salt mixture. Wrap the dish tightly with plastic wrap and cure in the refrigerator for 4 days.

Remove the fish from the salt mixture, rinse it under cold running water, and pat it dry. Lay the fish on a cutting board, skin side down, and use a sharp knife to cut thin slices on a steep bias without cutting through the skin. Vary the angle of your knife to make a wider slice. If you're slicing in advance, store the cut trout in a single layer between sheets of plastic wrap until you're ready to serve.

To make the lemon-caper crème fraîche, combine the crème fraîche, lemon zest and juice, capers, and poppy seeds in a bowl and mix well. Cover and refrigerate until you're ready to serve, up to 2 days.

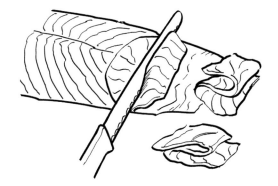

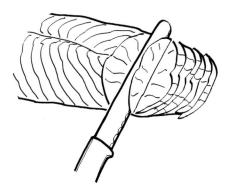

Recipe Continues

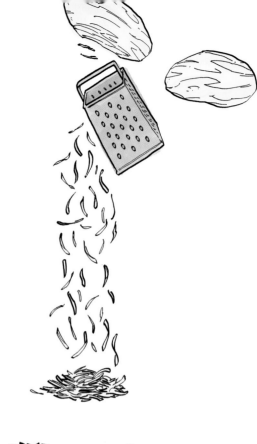

To make the hash browns, preheat your oven to 400°F. Bake the potatoes for 25 minutes (they should still be a little hard in the center when you take them out) and let them rest at room temperature until they're cool enough to handle. Peel the potatoes with a paring knife, then grate them into a large mixing bowl using the largest holes of a box grater.

Beat the egg in a small bowl and add the chopped scallions. Pour the egg into the grated potato and mix thoroughly with clean hands. Form the potato mixture into balls a bit smaller than a tennis ball. If you're not cooking them immediately, refrigerate the potato balls, covered, for up to 2 days.

Heat ⅛ inch of canola oil in a large skillet over medium-high heat. When the oil is hot, put the potato balls in the pan and gently flatten them with a spatula. Fry on one side until golden brown, about 4 minutes, then flip and brown the other side. Transfer the hash brown patties to a plate lined with paper towels and immediately sprinkle with salt on both sides.

To serve, lay a few slices of cured trout on top of each hash brown patty and finish with a dollop of lemon-caper crème fraîche.

The Night Before: *Slice the fish, layer with sheets of plastic wrap, and hold in the refrigerator. Mix the lemon-caper crème fraîche and hold in a covered container in the refrigerator. Make the potato balls for the hash browns and hold in a covered container in the refrigerator.*

"LEFTOVERS" FRITATTA

Serves 2

This frittata accommodates leftovers of all kinds—that too-little-for-lunch portion of pot-au-feu, the rest of the roasted vegetables, the final slice of last night's dry-aged rib eye (the one you had the restraint to put in the fridge instead of your mouth).

You did the real work last night; now you're just a few steps away from an easy and delicious dish.

Preheat your oven to 325°F. Beat the eggs thoroughly with a whisk, then fold in the leftovers and cheese. Add a bit of salt, adjusting for the saltiness of your cheese and your leftovers.

Heat a cast-iron skillet on the stovetop over high heat (see note). Add the canola oil and swirl it around so that the pan is evenly coated. When the oil starts to smoke, pour in the egg mixture all at once. Cook for 10 seconds, then transfer the pan to the oven. Bake the frittata for about 20 minutes, until it's firm to the touch.

Remove the skillet from the oven and set it aside to cool a bit. Turn the frittata out onto a cutting board, cut into wedges, and serve.

Note: *A heavy, well-seasoned cast-iron skillet—with its even heat and natural stick-resistance—is the thing to use here. The quantities in this recipe are scaled for an 8-inch pan.*

The Night Before: *Enjoy a fantastic dinner. Save some of it.*

**4 large
EGGS**

**1 cup
LEFTOVERS OF ANY KIND,**
chopped into bite-size pieces

**½ cup
GRATED CHEESE**
(such as cheddar, Parmesan, or Gruyère)

FINE SEA SALT

**1 tablespoon
CANOLA OIL**

IN PRAISE
OF THE
SCRAMBLE

The omelet is a pretty cool invention—an envelope made of eggs, fillable with just about anything. The problem with envelope eggs, though, is they often get overcooked along the way and their fillings are not really incorporated; they're just sitting in there, hopefully warm. Making a scramble instead of an omelet allows you to cook the eggs as soft or firm as you like and to incorporate the ingredients at the right moment (early for cheese, late for fresh herbs). In a bowl, they'll stay warm longer than an omelet ever would, making them perfect for a crowd.

Long live the scramble!

Note: *Quantities listed here serve 1. Multiply by the number of servings needed.*

Mushroom & Goat Cheese Scramble

**1 tablespoon
UNSALTED BUTTER**

**½ cup
roughly chopped cooked
MUSHROOMS**

**2
LARGE EGGS,
beaten**

FINE SEA SALT

**2 tablespoons
GOAT CHEESE**

Heat the butter in a small nonstick pan over medium-high heat. Add the mushrooms to the pan, stirring frequently, until they're hot. Turn the heat to high, pour in the beaten eggs, and season with salt. Scramble the eggs, removing the pan from the heat and stirring in the goat cheese just before the eggs have reached your desired degree of doneness.

The Night Before: *Chop and sauté the mushrooms and cool. Store in a covered container in the refrigerator.*

Cured Steelhead Trout Scramble

1 tablespoon
UNSALTED BUTTER

3 tablespoons
CHOPPED CURED STEELHEAD TROUT
(page 196), GRAVLAX,
OR SMOKED SALMON

2
LARGE EGGS,
beaten

2 tablespoons
CREAM CHEESE

1 tablespoon sliced
SCALLION

FINE SEA SALT

Heat the butter in a small nonstick pan over medium-high heat. Add the trout and cook, stirring frequently, until the fish is warmed through. Turn the heat to high, add the eggs, cream cheese, and scallion, and salt lightly (the fish will add some saltiness, too). Scramble the eggs, removing the pan from the heat just before they have reached your desired degree of doneness.

Pipérade & Merguez Scramble

1 tablespoon
UNSALTED BUTTER

2 tablespoons
PIPÉRADE
(page 90)

2 tablespoons diced cooked
MERGUEZ SAUSAGE OR OTHER
SPICY SAUSAGE

2
LARGE EGGS,
beaten

FINE SEA SALT

Heat the butter in a small nonstick pan over medium-high heat. Add the pipérade and merguez and cook, stirring, until they're hot. Turn the heat to high, add the eggs, and season with salt. Scramble, removing the pan from the heat just before the eggs have reached your desired degree of doneness.

The Night Before: *Prepare the pipérade, cool, and store in a covered container in the refrigerator. Cook the merguez, cool, and dice. Store in a covered container in the refrigerator.*

16 thick slices
BACON

2
SMALL APPLES,
any variety

½ cup
AIOLI
(page 4)

8 slices
BREAD
(preferably sourdough)

16 thin slices
SHARP CHEDDAR CHEESE

NONSTICK COOKING SPRAY

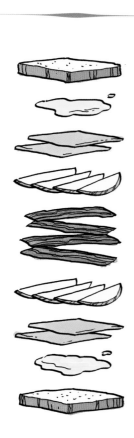

A-B-C
GRILLED CHEESE

Makes 4 sandwiches

That's apple-bacon-cheddar. The A could stand for aioli, too, as there should be a generous layer on both slices of bread. The best bread for this sandwich is a rustic sourdough loaf, but other kinds of bread are fine as long as you can cut it into slices that are about 6 inches long or wide, the length of a piece of cooked bacon.

Preheat your oven to 350°F. Lay out the bacon in a single layer on a rimmed baking sheet and bake to your ideal level of crispiness. Transfer the bacon to a plate lined with paper towels.

Peel the apples, if you like, or just wash and leave them unpeeled. Core the apples and cut them into thin slices.

To assemble each sandwich, spread a generous amount of aioli on two slices of bread. On the bottom slice, layer two slices of cheese, a few apple slices, four slices of bacon, more apple, then another two slices of cheese. Top with the second slice of bread.

Coat a griddle or sauté pan with cooking spray and heat over medium heat. Press the sandwiches into the hot pan. Cook until golden brown on one side, then flip to brown the second side. Lower the heat, if necessary, to get the cheese fully melted by the time the outside of the sandwich is toasted.

The Night Before: *Assemble the sandwiches and hold in a covered container in the refrigerator.*

GRAPEFRUIT & ENDIVE SALAD

Serves 4

This salad offers a refreshing counterpoint on a table laden with hearty brunch fare.

Cut the peel and white pith from the grapefruit with a chef's knife or paring knife. Slice the fruit into ¼-inch-thick wheels.

Trim the base off the endive and separate them into whole leaves. In a mixing bowl, grate the lime zest over the endive with a Microplane or other fine grater. Cut the lime in half and squeeze the juice over the endive. Toss gently with clean hands to evenly dress the leaves.

Arrange the endive and grapefruit wheels on a platter or individual plates. Drizzle with the olive oil and sprinkle with sea salt.

**2
GRAPEFRUIT**

**2 heads
BELGIAN ENDIVE**

**1
LIME**

**2 tablespoons
EXTRA-VIRGIN OLIVE OIL**

COARSE SEA SALT

CORDON BLEU

For the Fried Chicken

**8
BONELESS, SKIN-ON
CHICKEN THIGHS**

**2 cups
BUTTERMILK**

**4 sprigs
FRESH TARRAGON**

**4 cups
ALL-PURPOSE FLOUR**

**2 teaspoons
BLACK PEPPER,
plus more for seasoning**

FINE SEA SALT

**CANOLA OIL,
for frying**

For the Mornay Sauce

**2 tablespoons
UNSALTED BUTTER**

**3½ tablespoons
ALL-PURPOSE FLOUR**

**3 cups
WHOLE MILK**

**1 cup
HEAVY CREAM**

**4
WHOLE BLACK
PEPPERCORNS**

**2
WHOLE CLOVES**

**1
BAY LEAF**

**1 cup
GRATED
GRUYÈRE CHEESE**

To Serve

**8 slices
GRUYÈRE CHEESE**

**1 head
BIBB LETTUCE**

**2 tablespoons
BANYULS
VINAIGRETTE**
(page 46)

**8
CORNICHONS**

**8 slices
BENTON'S COUNTRY
HAM**

Special Equipment

**CANDY OR DEEP-FRY
THERMOMETER**

**4 (6-inch)
BAMBOO SKEWERS**

This variation on traditional chicken cordon bleu (an all-American classic with a French name) would make a great dinner, but at French Louie, we've found that it's just the kind of fried, cheesy goodness people want at brunch. We use another all-American classic in our version: salty, chewy ham from Benton's Smoky Mountain Country Hams in Tennessee. You can order it from them online, or substitute another dry-cured, country-style ham or prosciutto.

PREPARE THE CHICKEN

Put the chicken thighs in a large bowl, add the buttermilk and tarragon, cover, and refrigerate for at least 4 hours or overnight.

In a large mixing bowl, combine the flour, pepper, and a pinch of salt. Working one piece at a time, remove the chicken thighs from the buttermilk, allow to drain for a moment, and dredge in the seasoned flour. Transfer the floured chicken to a tray or plate, wrap with plastic, and refrigerate for at least 1 hour or until you're ready to fry. Cover the flour bowl and store in the refrigerator.

MAKE THE MORNAY SAUCE

Before you fry the chicken, make the sauce: In a medium saucepan, melt the butter over medium-low heat, then add the flour and whisk to form a paste. Cook for about 5 minutes, whisking frequently. Add the milk slowly, pouring in a thin stream while whisking constantly. Follow with the cream. Continue whisking while the mixture comes

to a simmer, then add the peppercorns, cloves, and bay leaf and turn the heat to low. Simmer for an additional 10 minutes, whisking occasionally. Remove from the heat and add the Gruyère cheese, whisking until it's fully incorporated. Strain the sauce through a fine-mesh sieve, press a piece of plastic wrap directly over its surface to prevent a skin from forming, and hold in a warm place until ready to serve.

FRY THE CHICKEN

Preheat your oven to 450°F and set a wire rack over a rimmed baking sheet to hold the cooked chicken. Dredge the chicken one more time in the bowl of reserved flour. Fill a large cast-iron skillet with 3-inch-high sides halfway with canola oil and heat over medium heat to 360°F on a candy thermometer. Drop the chicken thighs in the hot oil, making sure to leave a little space around each thigh (fry in two batches if the chicken won't all fit in the pan). When the chicken is golden brown and crispy on the bottom, carefully flip and continue

Recipe Continues

205

cooking until the other side until is golden, about 8 minutes total.

Remove a chicken thigh from the pan and test with a digital probe thermometer. The cooked chicken should have an internal temperature of 165°F. When done, transfer the chicken to the wire rack and season liberally with salt and pepper.

TO SERVE

Lay a slice of Gruyère on top of each chicken thigh and move the baking sheet to the oven. Take it out when the cheese is just melted, about 2 minutes.

Separate the Bibb lettuce into whole leaves. In a small bowl, gently toss the lettuce leaves in the vinaigrette and season with salt to taste.

Put two cornichons on each bamboo skewer. Spoon about ¼ cup of the Mornay sauce on each plate. On top of the sauce, layer a piece of chicken, 1 or 2 lettuce leaves (depending on their size), and a slice of ham. Top with a second layer of chicken, lettuce, and ham. Use the cornichon skewers to hold these towers of deliciousness together. Serve immediately.

The Night Before: *The day before, the chicken can be marinated in the buttermilk for 8 hours, then floured and held in a single layer on a rimmed baking sheet, covered, overnight in the refrigerator. In fact, the extra time with the flour will make for a crispier crust.*

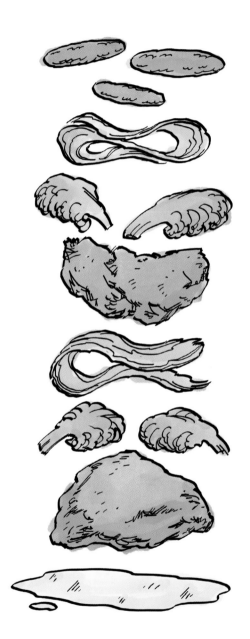

BREAKFAST SAUSAGE

Makes 15 sausage patties

The dried pears in this recipe bring a variety of texture that is often missing in a sausage patty, and their sweetness offsets the spicy-hot kick of the chile flakes.

Soften the dried pears in a bowl of warm water for a few minutes. Drain and dice the pears into ⅛-inch cubes. Put the pears in a large mixing bowl and add all the remaining ingredients (except the canola oil). Mix thoroughly with your hands or in a standing mixer on low speed with the paddle attachment. Cover the bowl and refrigerate the sausage mix for about an hour, until it's completely chilled.

Form the sausage mix into small patties about 2½ inches wide. Stack the patties on a plate, layered with wax paper. Cook immediately or cover with plastic wrap and refrigerate at least an hour, or until you're ready to cook. The sausage patties can also be frozen for up to 2 weeks.

Heat a sauté pan or griddle with a light coating of canola oil over medium-low heat. Brown the sausage patties slowly on both sides, about 4 minutes total, at which point they should be cooked through. Serve immediately.

1 cup
DRIED PEARS

2½ pounds
GROUND PORK

1
LARGE EGG,
beaten

¼ cup
CHOPPED FRESH SAGE

1 tablespoon
FRESH THYME LEAVES

2 teaspoons
RED CHILE FLAKES

2 teaspoons
FINE SEA SALT

1 teaspoon
GROUND GINGER

½ teaspoon
BLACK PEPPER

½ teaspoon
GROUND CINNAMON

¼ teaspoon
GROUND CLOVES

CANOLA OIL,
for sautéing

BUTTERMILK
BISCUITS

2 cups
BUTTERMILK

8 ounces
CREAM CHEESE,
at room temperature

4 cups
ALL-PURPOSE FLOUR,
plus more for dusting

4 teaspoons
BAKING POWDER

1 teaspoon
BAKING SODA

1 teaspoon
KOSHER SALT

16 tablespoons (2 sticks)
UNSALTED BUTTER,
frozen, plus
4 tablespoons (½ stick)
UNSALTED BUTTER,
melted

Makes about 12 biscuits

Like pancakes, biscuits are the stuff brunch reputations are built on. To avoid overworking the dough, you need to combine the ingredients as gently as possible, and mix them only to the point that they barely come together. Have faith: this lumpy mess will transform in the oven into flaky, golden biscuits. Perfection, and your renown as a biscuit maestro, will come with practice. Enjoy your biscuits with salted butter and jam or underneath Eggs Benedict (page 192), or make the World's Best Egg and Cheese by sandwiching cheesy scrambled eggs and bacon between the halves.

Preheat your oven to 425°F and line a rimmed baking sheet with parchment paper. In a large mixing bowl, whisk together the buttermilk and cream cheese until smooth. In a separate bowl, whisk together the flour, baking powder, baking soda, and salt.

Remove the butter from the freezer and grate on the coarse side of a box grater directly onto the dry ingredients. Pour the buttermilk mixture into the dry ingredients. Work quickly with your hands to loosely form the dough,

stopping when the ingredients are just barely combined. The finished biscuit dough should be lumpy, with visible pieces of butter in it.

Turn out the dough onto a heavily floured work surface. Dust the top of the dough with more flour and spread it out with your hands until it's about 1 inch thick. Cut the dough with a 2½- or 3-inch biscuit cutter, dipping the cutter first into flour before punching out each biscuit. (Flouring the cutter will give the biscuits straight sides and help them rise fully.)

Line up the biscuits side by side on the lined baking sheet. Leave no space between the biscuits, as they rise better when they're touching. Brush the tops of the biscuits with the melted butter and bake for 10 minutes. Rotate the pan and bake for a few more minutes, until the biscuits are evenly browned. Serve immediately, or cool and store in a covered container at room temperature for 24 hours. Reheat in a hot oven before serving.

GRITS

Serves 6

1 cup
STONE-GROUND GRITS
(Polenta or "quick grits" are acceptable substitutes, but not as good. Avoid instant grits like the uncle who gets drunk at every wedding.)

2 cups
WATER

4 cups
WHOLE MILK

1 tablespoon
UNSALTED BUTTER

½ cup crumbled
GOAT CHEESE

TABASCO SAUCE

FINE SEA SALT

Like its Italian cousin, polenta, grits are a soul-warming and versatile side dish that transcends the hot cereal category and the breakfast table. Put an egg on them in the morning, or serve under braised short ribs or a piece of grilled fish at dinner.

We know that grits belong to that category of beloved foods that give rise to strong feelings, particularly in the South. (In the Northeast, we prefer Quaker oatmeal in the morning, but no one gets that excited about it.) So be warned: these grits have goat cheese in them. This is either okay with you or it isn't. We've found that the tangy creaminess of goat cheese means you need less butter, so these will be lighter than the grits Mama made.

In a small bowl, soak the grits in the water for a minute. Pour off the excess water, along with any particles that have floated to the top.

In a medium saucepan, bring the milk and butter to a boil over medium heat. Pour the grits in slowly and reduce the heat to low. Simmer the grits for 20 minutes, stirring frequently to prevent sticking.

Whisk in the goat cheese. Season the grits with Tabasco and salt to taste and serve immediately.

SHORT RIB HASH

Serves 4

Braise a big batch of short ribs for dinner and save the leftovers to make this hearty hash a day or two later. The short ribs will be even better after they've cooled in their cooking liquid and spent some time in the refrigerator.

Preheat your oven to 350°F. Toss the diced potatoes with a little canola oil and spread them out in a single layer on a rimmed baking sheet. Roast the potatoes, stirring them from time to time to prevent sticking, until they're brown, about 15 minutes. Remove the potatoes from the oven and cool to room temperature.

Chop the short rib meat into rough chunks and combine in a bowl with the carrot, scallion, parsley, and cinnamon. Fold in the cooked potatoes.

Melt the butter in a large sauté pan over high heat. When the pan is hot and the butter starts to foam, add the hash and press it down into a ¾- to 1-inch layer covering the surface of the pan. Once the hash is hot and nicely browned on the bottom, give it a quick stir, season with salt to taste, and take the pan off the heat. Divide among four plates and top with eggs, any style.

The Night Before: *Chop the short ribs, roast and cool the potatoes, and grate the carrot. Mix them with the scallion, parsley, and cinnamon and store in a covered container in the refrigerator.*

1
LARGE RUSSET POTATO,
peeled and diced

CANOLA OIL,
for drizzling

3 to 4
BRAISED SHORT RIBS
(page 144) for 4 cups cooked meat

1
CARROT,
grated

2 tablespoons
CHOPPED SCALLION

2 tablespoons
CHOPPED FRESH FLAT-LEAF PARSLEY

1 teaspoon
GROUND CINNAMON

2 tablespoons
UNSALTED BUTTER

FINE SEA SALT

8
LARGE EGGS,
prepared however you'd like

BLOODY MARY

The Drink That Eats Like a Meal

The modern cocktail world accommodates all kinds of wild combinations, but this country-club standard holds the title for weirdest drink in the world, composed of ingredients from the kitchen—celery salt, Worcestershire sauce, hot sauce—that you'd never expect to meet at a bar. The Bloody Mary is the platypus of cocktails; it exists outside of the smooth continuum of evolution. Inexplicable, maybe, but at brunch it's just right.

Bloody Mary Bar

The past decade has seen the Bloody Mary expand from a single cocktail into a whole category of drinks, with endless variations on the original. For a brunch party, a do-it-yourself Bloody Mary bar, with an arsenal of base spirits, add-ins, and garnishes, allows your guests to invent their own signature Bloody. This setup is as much a party game as it is beverage service.

SPIRITS

There's no need to break the bank buying top-quality liquor for your Bloody Marys. The nuances of whatever liquor you use will be lost in all that tomato juice and spice. Like the wines you cook with, though, the base spirits you use for Bloody Marys should be palatable on their own (with one notable exception).

Vodka: This is the standard, and the exception to the aforementioned "palatability" rule, because vodka has no flavor that would come through in this drink. Use the cheap stuff.

Gin: A Bloody made with gin is called a Red Snapper, a drink invented at the King Cole Bar at the St. Regis Hotel in Manhattan. Classy! Go with a spicy "London dry" style gin, such as Beefeater, Boodles, Gordon's, or Tanqueray.

Tequila: Tequila turns your Mary into a Bloody Maria. Don't use aged tequilas, as they'll add an unwanted oakiness.

Whiskey: Bourbon adds a bit of sweetness to balance the spice. Alternatively, a float of good single-malt scotch is luxurious and will add a beautiful smoky note to your drink.

Note: A virgin Bloody Mary is known as A Bloody Shame—but perhaps morning drinkers shouldn't be so judgy. A short shot of the mix will kick-start your Sunday morning.

GARNISHES AND ADD-INS

Just about anything you can fit on the rim of a glass or on a skewer is fair game for a Bloody Mary garnish. Let your imagination run wild.

Celery: This is, of course, the classic. It looks great and is fun to crunch on.

Olives: Briny, salty, bitter olives are an ideal match for this drink. Buy different types and thread them onto skewers, or put them out in bowls so your guests can drop them in.

Pickles: Any of the pickles in our Pantry section (pages 26–29) would work great at your Bloody bar. In a pinch, grab good pickles at the store. Cut them lengthwise in quarters for spears, or slice them into thin rounds to layer on a skewer with other garnishes.

Italian Antipasti: At Buttermilk Channel, we serve a rosemary-infused vodka Bloody, garnished with an antipasto skewer: a slice of soppressata, a chunk of salty Italian cheese, and an olive—all sourced from Caputo's, the legendary Italian grocer down the street. Put out an array of dry sausages and cheeses, and some roasted and marinated vegetables like peppers and eggplant to keep the vegetarians happy.

Oysters: Choose oysters with shells large enough to sit on top of the glass without falling in. Scrub the shells well before serving. Open the oysters in the kitchen and put them out, a few at a time, on a bed of crushed ice.

Bagel Chips: These make for a nice crunchy-salty accent, and they fit neatly over a straw. At French Louie, we pair this garnish with "Everything Bagel" Salt (see below).

Hot Sauces: Our recipe calls for Tabasco and is pretty hot already, but plenty of people will want their Bloody even hotter. In addition to a bottle of Tabasco, put out something mild, like Frank's, and something crazy hot, like a Mexican habanero sauce.

Beer: A float of stout is a surprisingly nice contrast to the spicy, tart notes in this drink. A lighter beer, like a pilsner, is good for a chaser.

SALT RIMS

A rim on a cocktail is the first thing that hits your lips and should be a burst of flavor and texture. Use kosher salt. About ½ cup of any of these should be enough for up to ten people:

Chile-Lime Salt: Combine ½ cup salt, 1 teaspoon chopped jalapeño, and the finely grated zest of 1 lime in the bowl of a food processor. Pulse until combined.

Paprika Salt: Mix ½ cup salt with 2 tablespoons paprika. Smoked paprika and sweet Hungarian paprika are both charmers on a rim.

"Everything Bagel" Salt: Mix ½ cup salt with 1 teaspoon each sesame seeds, poppy seeds, dried onion flakes, and dried garlic flakes.

Rye Toast Salt: Dry 2 slices of seeded rye bread in your oven at 200°F for 2 hours. Blend thoroughly in a food processor. Mix the bread crumbs with an equal volume of salt. Optional: add 1 teaspoon caraway seeds for extra rye bread flavor.

SETTING THE TABLE

On a table large enough to accommodate your Bloody Mary bar, lay out the following items, more or less in this order from left to right, so people can move down the table as they build their drinks.

- 11- to 13-ounce glasses
- Plain kosher salt and flavored salts in shallow dishes, alongside small wedges of lemon or lime for moistening the glass rims
- Ice in a bucket or bowl, with a spoon or tongs
- Cocktail jiggers to measure out the booze
- Bottles of spirits
- Pitchers of Bloody mix
- Cocktail stirrers or swizzle sticks
- Straws (optional, especially with a rim, but most people prefer them)
- Pepper mill filled with black peppercorns
- Garnishes in bowls with tongs, forks, or spoons for serving
- 4- to 6-inch cocktail skewers (for holding garnishes too small to balance on the rim of the glass)
- Ice bucket with beer bottles

CORPSE REVIVER NO. 2

THE FANCIEST BRUNCH COCKTAIL OF THEM ALL

This is the most elegant of the "hair of the dog"
hangover cures. Refreshing and pleasantly bitter, it packs a punch. This
drink looks best in a 5- or 6-ounce cocktail coupe
(the old-fashioned Champagne glass that elicits the inevitable
story about Marie Antoinette's breasts), but a rocks
glass will do in a pinch.

Serves 1

1 ounce gin

1 ounce Cocchi Americano or Lillet Blanc

1 ounce Cointreau

1 ounce fresh lemon juice

Dash absinthe

Orange twist, for garnish

Chill your coupe or rocks glass in the freezer or by filling it with ice and water while you mix the drink. Measure the gin, Cocchi Americano, Cointreau, lemon juice, and absinthe into the glass of your shaker, then fill the glass about three-quarters full with ice. Shake vigorously for about 20 seconds. Strain into the chilled coupe glass or a rocks glass with ice, and garnish with the orange twist.

Bloody Mary

Makes 5 to 7 drinks

It is possible to whip up a batch of Bloody Marys from scratch in just a few minutes, but if you foresee Bloodys in your future, they'll taste better if the ingredients get to mingle for a few hours.

For the Bloody Mary Mix

24 ounces
TOMATO JUICE
(we prefer Sacramento brand)

½ cup
LEMON JUICE
(2 to 3 lemons)

5 tablespoons
PREPARED HORSERADISH

1½ tablespoons
WORCESTERSHIRE SAUCE

1¼ teaspoons
TABASCO SAUCE

1½ teaspoons
BLACK PEPPER

1¼ teaspoons
CELERY SALT

To Complete the Drink

RIMS, GARNISHES, AND ADD-INS

ICE

SPIRITS

Combine all the ingredients for the mix and refrigerate in an airtight container for at least 6 hours or up to 4 days.

When ready to serve:

- If using a salt rim, first wet the rim of an 11- to 13-ounce glass with a wedge of lemon or lime, then dredge the rim in one of the salt plates.

- Add ice cubes up to the top of the glass, being careful not to disturb your rim.

- Using a jigger, measure 2 ounces of your selected liquor.

- Pour in Bloody Mary mix to about ½ inch below the top of the glass (1 inch below, if you're planning on a float).

- Stir the drink with a stirrer or swizzle stick.

- Pick up a cocktail skewer and select your garnishes. All the garnishes in our list play nicely together, so you can't go wrong. Larger garnishes like celery sticks and pickle spears may be sunk right into the drinks without a skewer.

- If desired, top with a float of beer or liquor, extra dash of hot sauce, or grind of pepper. Enjoy, and repeat (responsibly).

Recipes
FOR

POPOVERS GOUGÈRES PIES TARTS
CORNBREAD PROFITEROLES

BAKED

—— ◇ ——

THERE IS EXTRA KINDNESS in a meal that begins and ends with something freshly baked.

At French Louie, when we see an old friend for the first time in a while, we'll bring them out a basket of cheesy, fragrant gougères to start their meal. When brunch lines get crazy at Buttermilk Channel, we find that a platter of warm sticky buns has a transformative effect on even the hangriest parties. Toast is nice, but a buttermilk biscuit with jam and butter turns a plate of eggs into a luxurious feast.

Producing desserts, breads, and other savory baked goods for hundreds of customers a day is about as much of a challenge in our cramped kitchens as it would be in yours. Out of necessity, our baking recipes are relatively simple and efficient, requiring a minimum of bowls and very little special equipment. Our ovens spend most of their days roasting vegetables and simmering long, slow braises, leaving barely enough room to bake a biscuit, let alone twenty dozen of them. Most of these items will hold nicely for at least a day or two—so unlike our pastry chefs, you won't have to get up at four in the morning to get your baking done.

POPOVERS
WITH HONEY & SEA SALT 224

GOUGÈRES 226

PIE DOUGH 227

DELICATA SQUASH TART 228

CORNBREAD
WITH CHILE-LIME BUTTER 230

LEMON-POPPY BUTTERMILK CAKE 232

PINEAPPLE TARTE TATIN
WITH TOASTED COCONUT ICE CREAM 234

OVER THE
TOP

244

RUM RAISIN TORTE 237

BANANAS FOSTER PROFITEROLES 238

CHOCOLATE POTS DE CRÈME
WITH ORANGE CRÈME FRAÎCHE 240

TARTE AU FROMAGE
WITH HUCKLEBERRY & LIME 242

POPOVERS
WITH
HONEY & SEA SALT

NONSTICK COOKING SPRAY

1½ cups
ALL-PURPOSE FLOUR

FINE SEA SALT

6
LARGE EGGS

2 cups
WHOLE MILK

4 tablespoons (½ stick)
UNSALTED BUTTER,
melted

HONEY,
for drizzling

COARSE SEA SALT,
for garnishing

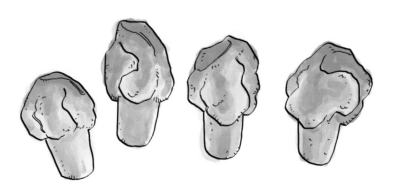

The British call them Yorkshire puddings and serve them alongside roast beef, but in America we call them popovers, and at Buttermilk Channel this is how you start your meal. The secret to making popovers rather than droopy pop-unders is to get the pan super-hot before adding the batter and to allow a nice crust to form before you start poking impatiently at them.

Preheat your oven to 425°F. Thoroughly coat the cups of a muffin tin with cooking spray and preheat it in the oven for 10 minutes.

Combine the flour and a pinch of salt in a small bowl and mix to combine. In a standing mixer with the whisk attachment, beat the eggs until they're light and fluffy. Reduce the speed to low and beat in the milk, followed by the melted butter. Then gradually add the flour and salt mixture. Transfer the batter to a vessel with a spout for easy pouring into the muffin tin.

Carefully remove the hot muffin tin from the oven and place it on a rimmed baking sheet. Work quickly to fill the cups halfway with batter. Put the baking sheet on the middle shelf of the oven and bake the popovers for 25 to 30 minutes, resisting the urge to open the oven door for at least the first 20 minutes. When they're finished baking, the popovers should be golden brown and sound hollow when you give them a quick tap.

Turn the popovers out of the muffin tin. While the tin is still hot, coat it again with cooking spray, fill with batter, and bake off the next batch. Repeat until the batter is used up.

Serve the popovers while still warm, or allow them to cool and store in an airtight container at room temperature for up to 3 days. When ready to serve, warm the popovers in a 350°F oven for about 5 minutes. Drizzle with honey, sprinkle with coarse sea salt, and serve immediately.

Note: *We use a muffin tin with cups that hold 3½ ounces (not quite ½ cup). You may use a tin with larger cups to make fewer, but larger, popovers.*

GOUGÈRES

1 cup
WATER

8 tablespoons (1 stick)
UNSALTED BUTTER

1 cup plus 2 tablespoons
ALL-PURPOSE FLOUR

½ teaspoon
FINE SEA SALT

4
EXTRA-LARGE EGGS

½ cup
**GRATED COTIJA CHEESE OR
PECORINO ROMANO**

½ cup
GRATED GRUYÈRE CHEESE

BAKED

Makes 24 gougères

Gougères are to French Louie as popovers are to Buttermilk Channel: addictive, savory pastry puffs to pop in your mouth while you're waiting for dinner to be ready. You probably wouldn't find cotija in Burgundy (the gougère's ancestral home), but a crumble of this tangy-salty Mexican cheese is the secret weapon in this cocktail snack.

Preheat your oven to 375°F and line a baking sheet with parchment paper.

Combine the water and butter in a small saucepan and bring it to a boil over medium heat. Reduce the heat to low and, using a wooden spoon, quickly stir in the flour and salt all at once. Cook for 3 to 4 minutes, stirring constantly, until the dough comes together into a ball and a skin forms on the bottom of the pan. Remove the pan from the heat and allow it to cool slightly. Beat in one egg at a time with the wooden spoon, fully incorporating each egg before adding the next one. Beat in the cotija and Gruyère cheeses.

Transfer the dough to a piping bag with no tip attached and pipe the dough onto the lined baking sheet in small mounds about the diameter of a quarter, spacing them about 2 inches apart. Bake for 20 to 30 minutes, resisting the urge to open the oven door for a peek during the first 20 minutes. The gougères are done when they've doubled in size and are golden brown. Serve immediately or cool completely and reheat in a hot oven right before serving. Gougères will last for a day if cooled fully and stored in an airtight container at room temperature.

PIE DOUGH

*Makes enough dough for
2 (12-inch) rounds*

Don't be intimidated—it's going to turn out great. The key here is to keep things cold. The chunks of cold butter are what will make it flaky.

Combine the flour, a pinch of salt, and the cold butter cubes in the bowl of a food processor. Pulse the food processor until the butter has broken into pea-size lumps. Pour in the cold water and pulse a few more times. Turn out the dough onto a work surface and form it into a ball. Wrap the dough in plastic and refrigerate for at least 1 hour before rolling out for pie crust.

1⅔ cups
ALL-PURPOSE FLOUR

FINE SEA SALT

16 tablespoons (2 sticks)
UNSALTED BUTTER,
cut into 1-inch cubes and chilled

⅓ cup
COLD WATER

DELICATA SQUASH TART

CANOLA OIL,
for brushing

2
DELICATA SQUASH

FINE SEA SALT

1 recipe
PIE DOUGH
(page 227)

1
LARGE EGG,
beaten

2 cups
BUTTERMILK RICOTTA
(page 14)

4 tablespoons (½ stick)
UNSALTED BUTTER

¼ cup
BALSAMIC VINEGAR

2 tablespoons
GRATED
PECORINO ROMANO

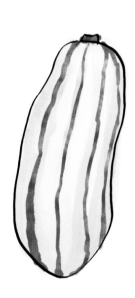

Just about any squash would work for this recipe, but a creamy delicata can be served with its tender, pretty rind intact, which makes for a great-looking tart.

Preheat your oven to 375°F and brush a rimmed baking sheet with canola oil. Cut the squash into ½-inch-thick rounds, cleaning out any pulp and seeds as you go. Lay the squash in a single layer on the prepared baking sheet. Brush the exposed surface of the squash with a light coating of canola oil and season with salt. Roast the squash until it's soft and lightly browned, about 15 minutes. Remove from the oven and set aside.

On a floured work surface, roll out the pie dough to ⅛-inch thickness. Use an 8- to 10-inch plate as a guide to cut out your round. (To make several individual tarts, use a small saucer; see note.) Lay the dough round on a rimmed baking sheet and brush with the beaten egg. Bake until golden brown, 15 to 20 minutes. Remove the tart shell from the oven and allow it to cool completely on the baking sheet.

Raise the temperature of the oven to 400°F. Gently spread a layer of ricotta on the tart shell, covering its entire surface. Shingle the roasted squash rounds on top of the ricotta. Drop a few more dollops of ricotta on top of the squash and return the baking sheet to the oven. Bake the tart until the ricotta just starts to brown, 8 to 10 minutes. Remove the tart from the oven, allow it to cool slightly, then transfer it to a plate.

Meanwhile, in a small saucepan, melt the butter over medium heat and continue to cook until it becomes browned and has a nutty aroma. Drizzle the tart with the brown butter and balsamic vinegar. Sprinkle with salt, top with the grated Pecorino Romano, and serve.

Note: *You may choose to make several individual-size tarts rather than one large tart. The quantities of ricotta and squash are approximate. No two squash in this world are exactly the same, so use your judgment to decide how much ricotta and squash looks right on each tart.*

CORNBREAD
WITH
CHILE-LIME BUTTER

◆

For the Chile-Lime Butter

8 tablespoons (1 stick)
UNSALTED BUTTER,
at room temperature

3
PICKLED CHERRY
PEPPERS,
halved, seeded, and minced

GRATED ZEST AND
JUICE OF 1 LIME

1 teaspoon
FINE SEA SALT

For the Cornbread

1¼ cups
ALL-PURPOSE FLOUR

¾ cup
YELLOW CORNMEAL

¼ cup
SUGAR

2 teaspoons
BAKING POWDER

½ teaspoon
FINE SEA SALT

1 cup
WHOLE MILK

¼ cup
AIOLI (page 4) OR
MAYONNAISE

¼ cup
CANOLA OIL,
plus more for greasing

1
LARGE EGG

2 cups
CRUMBLED FETA

◆

Cornbread is one of those foods that are rarely as good as people expect them to be. Our recipe has a few nontraditional ingredients that set it apart from the usual arid, flavorless loaves. Feta adds tangy acidity, and aioli is a nice trick to guarantee the moistness you hope for—but don't often find—in a cornbread.

To make the chile-lime butter, in a small bowl, mix the softened butter, minced peppers, lime zest and juice, and salt until fully combined. Cover and refrigerate, taking it out to soften 30 minutes before serving.

To make the cornbread, preheat your oven to 400°F. Whisk together the flour, cornmeal, sugar, baking powder, and salt in a medium bowl. In a separate bowl, whisk together the milk, aioli, oil, and egg until smooth. Add the wet ingredients to the dry and stir until fully incorporated. Stir in the crumbled feta.

Grease a 9-inch cast-iron skillet with canola oil and heat over medium heat. When the pan begins to smoke, turn off the heat and pour in the batter. Transfer the pan to the middle shelf of the oven. Bake for 20 to 25 minutes, until the cornbread is golden brown and a toothpick inserted into its center comes out clean. Remove from the pan and serve warm, with the softened chile-lime butter on top.

For the Cake

1 cup
VEGETABLE SHORTENING

8 tablespoons (1 stick)
UNSALTED BUTTER

2½ cups
SUGAR

4
LARGE EGGS

3½ cups
ALL-PURPOSE FLOUR

½ teaspoon
FINE SEA SALT

1 teaspoon
LEMON EXTRACT

1 cup
BUTTERMILK

½ teaspoon
BAKING SODA

1 tablespoon
HOT WATER

1 tablespoon
POPPY SEEDS

For the Lemon Syrup

GRATED ZEST AND JUICE OF 1 LEMON

½ cup
SUGAR

½ cup
WATER

LEMON-POPPY
BUTTERMILK
CAKE

This is a pretty Bundt cake—golden yellow and speckled with poppy seeds. It's the kind of cake everyone shaves away at until there's nothing left. Put it out as a sweet option at brunch or serve for dessert.

Preheat your oven to 325°F. Grease and flour a 12-cup (10-inch) Bundt pan.

In a standing mixer with a paddle attachment, cream the shortening, butter, and sugar on medium speed until light and fluffy. On a slower speed, beat in the eggs, one at a time, making sure that each egg has been incorporated before adding the next.

In a small bowl, sift together the flour and salt. With the mixer on low speed, pour in about half of the flour mixture and allow it to incorporate completely. Add the lemon extract and about half of the buttermilk and allow that to incorporate. Repeat with the remaining flour and the remaining buttermilk. Dissolve the baking soda in the hot water and mix it in, followed by the poppy seeds.

Pour the batter into the prepared Bundt pan. Bake for about 1 hour and 15 minutes, until a toothpick inserted in the center comes out clean. Let the cake cool for 10 minutes before turning out onto a plate.

Meanwhile, combine the ingredients for the lemon syrup in a small saucepan over medium heat. Cook, stirring often, until the sugar is fully dissolved.

Spoon or brush the hot lemon syrup over the cake while it is still warm. Let cool completely before serving.

PINEAPPLE TARTE TATIN

WITH
TOASTED COCONUT
ICE CREAM

*For the Toasted Coconut
Ice Cream*

**2 cups
WHOLE MILK**

**2 cups
HEAVY CREAM**

**10
EXTRA-LARGE EGG
YOLKS**

**¾ cup
GRANULATED SUGAR**

**½ cup
UNSWEETENED
TOASTED COCONUT**

**1 teaspoon
FINE SEA SALT**

For the Dough

**1½ cups
ALL-PURPOSE FLOUR**

**2 tablespoons
GRANULATED SUGAR**

**1 teaspoon
FINE SEA SALT**

**16 tablespoons (2 sticks)
UNSALTED BUTTER,**
cut into ½-inch cubes and
chilled

**2 tablespoons
COLD WATER**

For the Rum Butter Sauce

**1 packed cup
DARK BROWN SUGAR**

**½ teaspoon
FINE SEA SALT**

**16 tablespoons (2 sticks)
UNSALTED BUTTER,**
at room temperature

**1½ tablespoons
HONEY**

**2 tablespoons
DARK RUM**

**2 tablespoons
HEAVY CREAM**

For the Tarte

**1
PINEAPPLE**

Special Equipment

ICE CREAM MAKER

This recipe is a marriage of two of the world's great inverted pastries—the American pineapple upside-down cake and the French tarte tatin. The point of baking upside-down is to get the fruit, rather than the crust, on the bottom of the pan, where it can caramelize and get all bittersweet and nutty. The dark rum and brown sugar in the rum butter sauce add further layers of caramelized flavors.

TOASTED COCONUT ICE CREAM

Scald the milk and cream in a small saucepan over medium heat. Prepare an ice water bath. In a mixing bowl, whisk together the egg yolks and sugar. Slowly pour the hot milk and cream into the egg yolk mixture, whisking constantly. Pour the contents of the bowl back into the saucepan and cook over low heat, stirring frequently, until the mixture thickens to the point that it will coat the back of a spoon. Remove the pan from the heat and place it directly in an ice water bath. Stir the mixture frequently until it's completely cool, then stir in the coconut and salt. Process in an ice cream maker following the manufacturer's instructions.

DOUGH

Combine the flour, sugar, salt, and cold butter cubes in the bowl of a standing mixer with the paddle attachment. Mix on low speed, drizzling in the cold water slowly, just until the dough comes together. Form the dough into a ball and wrap in plastic. Refrigerate the dough for at least 1 hour or overnight.

On a lightly floured surface, roll out the chilled dough to ¼-inch thickness. Place a 10-inch tart pan over the dough and use a paring knife to cut a circle to match the diameter of the pan. Transfer the dough round to a plate, cover with plastic wrap, and refrigerate for at least 30 minutes or until ready to use.

RUM BUTTER SAUCE

Combine the brown sugar, salt, and butter in the bowl of a standing mixer with the paddle attachment. Cream on high speed until the mixture is light and fluffy. Reduce to low speed and slowly mix in the honey, rum, and heavy cream. Set aside until ready to use.

Recipe Continues

235

TO ASSEMBLE

Preheat your oven to 375°F.

Using a chef's knife or serrated knife, remove the top and bottom of the pineapple. Stand the fruit upright and trim away its bark. Cut the pineapple lengthwise into quarters and cut away the fibrous core. Cut the quarters into ⅛-inch-thick slices.

Spread ⅓ cup of the rum butter sauce evenly around the bottom of your 10-inch tart pan. Shingle the pineapple slices in a circle around the bottom of the pan. Repeat, forming a second layer of pineapple. In the center of the round of dough, cut out a dime-size hole to allow some steam to escape while the tart is cooking. Lay the dough on top of the pineapple and press it down gently. Place the tart on a rimmed baking sheet and bake for 25 minutes, or until the crust is golden brown.

Remove the tart from the oven and allow it to cool for 5 minutes. Carefully flip the tart over onto a plate so that the fruit side is up. Show your guests how pretty this thing is before slicing it and topping with scoops of toasted coconut ice cream.

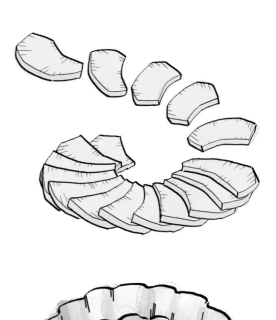

RUM RAISIN
TORTE

Serve 8 to 10

Remember how grown-up and sophisticated you felt the first time you tried, and loved, rum raisin ice cream? That's how this cake will make you feel. You've still got it. You have great taste in cookbooks, too.

Preheat your oven to 350°F. Grease a 12-inch tart pan and line the bottom with parchment paper.

In a standing mixer with the paddle attachment, combine the almond paste and sugar and mix until it resembles wet sand. Add the butter and continue mixing until it's smooth and uniform. Mix in the eggs, one at a time, followed by the vanilla.

In a separate bowl, whisk together the almond flour, baking powder, and salt. Pour the dry ingredients into the mixer and mix until smooth. Then fold in the raisins and sliced almonds.

Pour the batter into the prepared tart pan, place the tart pan on a rimmed baking sheet, and transfer it to the middle shelf of the oven. Bake for 10 minutes, then rotate the pan 180 degrees and bake for another 15 minutes, or until a toothpick inserted into the center comes out clean. Remove the torte from the oven and allow it to cool completely in the pan.

Cover the surface of the pan with a plate and, holding the bottom of the pan, flip the torte onto the plate. Lift off the pan and peel away the parchment paper. Evenly brush or spoon the rum over the surface of the torte. Dust with confectioners' sugar and slice into wedges to serve.

½ cup
ALMOND PASTE

¾ cup
GRANULATED SUGAR

9 tablespoons
UNSALTED BUTTER,
at room temperature,
cut into ½-inch cubes

3
LARGE EGGS

¼ teaspoon
VANILLA EXTRACT

1 cup
ALMOND FLOUR

1 teaspoon
BAKING POWDER

½ teaspoon
FINE SEA SALT

1 cup
BLACK RAISINS

½ cup
SLICED ALMONDS

½ cup
DARK RUM

CONFECTIONERS' SUGAR

BANANAS FOSTER

PROFITEROLES

For the Profiteroles

1 cup
WATER

8 tablespoons (1 stick)
UNSALTED BUTTER

1 cup
ALL-PURPOSE FLOUR

½ teaspoon
FINE SEA SALT

1 tablespoon plus 2 teaspoons
GRANULATED SUGAR

4
EXTRA-LARGE EGGS

For the Sauce

2 tablespoons
UNSALTED BUTTER

¼ packed cup
LIGHT BROWN SUGAR

2
RIPE BANANAS,
cut into ¼-inch-thick slices

¼ cup
BOURBON

½ teaspoon
FINE SEA SALT

To Serve

VANILLA ICE CREAM

Profiteroles are the sweet side of pâte à choux, the same magical French pastry used to make our Gougères (page 226). Bananas Foster was created at Brennan's in New Orleans's French Quarter, so further Frenchification is definitely appropriate.

Preheat your oven to 375°F and line a baking sheet with parchment paper.

To make the profiteroles, combine the water and butter in a small saucepan and bring it to a boil. Reduce the heat to low and, using a wooden spoon, quickly stir in the flour, salt, and 1 tablespoon of the sugar. Cook, stirring constantly, for 3 to 4 minutes, until the dough comes together into a ball and a skin forms on the bottom of the pan. Remove the dough from the heat and allow it to cool slightly. With the wooden spoon, beat in one egg at a time, fully incorporating each egg before adding the next one.

Transfer the dough to a piping bag with no tip attached and pipe the dough onto the lined baking sheet in small mounds about the diameter of a quarter, spacing them about 2 inches apart. Sprinkle the mounds with the remaining 2 teaspoons of sugar. Bake for 20 to 30 minutes, resisting the urge to open the oven door for the first 20 minutes. The profiteroles are done when they have doubled in size and are golden brown. Remove them from the oven and allow them to cool on the baking sheet.

To make the sauce, melt the butter and sugar in a medium sauté pan over medium heat. Toss in the sliced bananas and cook for a minute or so, stirring constantly. Add the bourbon, turn the heat up to high, and shake the pan to flambé. Simmer the bananas until the flames subside, add the salt, and give the pan a good stir.

To serve, cut the profiteroles in half, separating the top and bottom. Fill the base of each profiterole with a scoop of ice cream and cap with the profiterole tops. Spoon the bananas Foster sauce generously over the top and serve immediately.

CHOCOLATE
POTS DE CRÈME

with Orange Crème Fraîche

3 ounces
MILK CHOCOLATE

2 ounces
**BITTERSWEET
CHOCOLATE**

1¾ cups
HEAVY CREAM

¼ cup
DARK MOLASSES

1 teaspoon
GROUND CINNAMON

FINE SEA SALT

4
LARGE EGG YOLKS

2 tablespoons
DARK RUM

1 cup
CRÈME FRAÎCHE

**GRATED ZEST OF
1 ORANGE**

Special Equipment

6-ounce
**OVEN-SAFE CUSTARD
CUPS**

Serves 6 to 8

This pot de crème is one of the most popular desserts we've served at French Louie. Molasses, dark rum, and chocolate are just sexy together. Sing this recipe in your best Barry White voice.

Preheat your oven to 325°F. Melt the chocolates together in a metal bowl set over a saucepan of simmering water. Set the melted chocolate aside in a warm place until ready to use.

In a small saucepan, mix the cream, molasses, cinnamon, and a pinch of salt and scald over medium heat. Remove the pan from the heat and let the cream cool slightly, about 5 minutes. In a bowl, stir the egg yolks with a wooden spoon until smooth. Gradually mix the cream into the yolks. Slowly add this mixture to the melted chocolate, along with the rum, and stir until smooth. Portion about 5 ounces into each custard cup.

Line a baking dish with a kitchen towel and place the filled custard cups on the towel to hold them steady. Fill the dish with hot water about halfway up the sides of the cups, cover tightly with aluminum foil, and carefully place it on the middle shelf of the oven. Bake the pots de crème until they're almost fully set but still a bit wobbly in the center, 15 to 20 minutes. Remove the baking dish from the oven, uncover, and allow the pots de crème to cool in the water bath. Transfer the pots de crème to the refrigerator to chill completely.

When ready to serve, in a small bowl, whisk together the crème fraîche and orange zest until soft peaks form. Top each pot de crème with the crème fraîche and serve.

TARTE
AU FROMAGE
WITH
Huckleberry & Lime

For the Cracker Crust

**NONSTICK COOKING
SPRAY**

1¼ sleeves
SALTINE CRACKERS

6 tablespoons
UNSALTED BUTTER,
melted

1 tablespoon
SUGAR

For the Filling

1½ cups
CRÈME FRAÎCHE

½ cup
GREEK YOGURT

8 ounces
CREAM CHEESE

8 ounces
GOAT CHEESE

3
EXTRA-LARGE EGGS

1 cup
SUGAR

1 teaspoon
VANILLA EXTRACT

**GRATED ZEST OF
1 LIME**

PINCH FINE SEA SALT

To Serve

**GRATED ZEST OF
1 LIME**

HUCKLEBERRY JAM
(page 24)

Special Equipment

10-inch
**TART PAN WITH
REMOVABLE BOTTOM**

Don't call it a cheesecake. It's French.

Preheat your oven to 300°F and coat the inside of the tart pan with cooking spray. In the bowl of a food processor, combine the crackers, melted butter, and sugar and process until well combined. Pour the cracker mixture into the prepared tart pan and use your hands to press it into the bottom and up the sides. Refrigerate for 10 minutes, or until the crust is firm to the touch. Bake for 10 minutes. Set aside to cool.

Lower the oven temperature to 275°F. Combine all the filling ingredients in a food processor and process until smooth. Pour the filling into the cooled crust. Bake until the edges are set but the center is still a bit wobbly, about 25 minutes (check after 20 minutes). Allow the tart to cool to room temperature, then refrigerate until cold, at least 2 hours.

Gently remove the tart from the pan and sprinkle the lime zest over the top. Slice and serve with a generous spoonful of huckleberry jam.

OVER THE TOP

We *love* a celebration.

  We've toasted Oscar and Grammy nominations, spots on the bestseller list, raises and promotions, and long-overdue letters of resignation. It's a boy! It's a girl! It's a puppy!

  Special occasions are a green light for us to go over the top, to do a little more than is strictly necessary. Which is just the way we like it.

  We look forward to our friend Lucy's birthday each year. She's our absolute favorite eight-year-old, a brilliant, funny, curious kid with playground energy and a mouth like a gun moll in an old gangster movie. She has lovely parents, too, but a kid like that tends to steal the show. When Lucy comes in for dinner, we all have to remember that we've got orders to take, customers to seat, and drinks to make, so we can't spend the entire night solving riddles, playing hangman, or losing Harry Potter trivia contests. Of course, we're all competing to be the one Lucy loves the best.

  Julio and Deb are in charge of Lucy's birthday cake. As waiters, baking cakes is not in their job description, but there's no way the pastry chef is getting her hands on this one. Lucy's eighth birthday cake was the best yet, a marvel of engineering that left the previous year's cupcake tower in the dust: eight layers, each a different color of the rainbow, and purple frosting, topped by a blaze of sparklers that imperiled our eyelashes and the lampshades on the chandelier. When the cake was cut, its most exciting feature–a booby trap of candy at its core–poured out onto the table. It was, as they say, a lot. We're not sure how they're going to top that one next year.

  Kids love it when you go over the top; grown-ups sometimes need a bit of a shove. Our friend Phil came in for a quiet dinner on his birthday; he had no idea we'd conspired with his wife to fill the room with far-flung friends and family. That surprise was on him–but everyone in the room was shocked when the eight-piece brass band burst in blowing a swinging "Happy Birthday." We ushered in Phil's fiftieth with a march down Huntington Street in the New Orleans second line tradition–a surprise for our neighbors as well.

  Exploding cakes and brass bands aren't everyone's style, and not every dinner requires an over-the-top celebration. Maybe you're there to gaze into the eyes of a new flame, to negotiate a raise with your boss, or to catch up with an old friend. On those occasions, we'll fade into the background, bring you a meal, and save the chitchat for next time. Some customers always prefer to be left alone. If you fall into that category, rest assured that we love serving you, too, and will respect your privacy.

  But please know: if your inner eight-year-old does show up, we'll be ready with your birthday cake.

Recipes

FOR

MANHATTAN NEGRONI MARTINI

FRENCH 75 MARGARITA

COCKTAILS

—— ◆ ——

THERE'S NOTHING ON EARTH like a cocktail to mark the end of work and the beginning of fun.

Whether you've bellied up to someone else's bar or are making yourself a drink at home, the sound of ice hitting a glass is the signal that says it's time to relax. That drink doesn't even need liquor—a few special ingredients, a nice glass, and a pretty garnish will do the trick.

Just as the bars at the front of our restaurants allow us to properly welcome our customers, an opening round of drinks is a luxurious way to greet your guests at home. Whether it's salt-rimmed margaritas, frosty mint juleps, or lemony Arnold Palmers, that tray of drinks sets the tone for a lovely time together.

THE MANHATTAN 260

VARIATION: THE SAUL PANZER 261

THE NEGRONI 262

VARIATION: THE FOX 8 263

THE GIN MARTINI 264

THE FRENCH 75 266

VARIATION: THE HONEYSUCKLE ROSE 267

THE MARGARITA 268

VARIATION: THE CHESPIRITO 269

MAKING A TWIST 257

HOLD THE BOOZE 265

SETTING UP A HOME BAR 252

Setting Up a Home Bar

There's no need to overcomplicate your home bar, as long as you have the components and tools to make the drink you want when you want it. Our bartenders need to be ready for just about any cocktail request someone might throw at them; at home, you can get away with a far more limited menu.

Select three or four of your favorites and set yourself up with the gear and ingredients to make those drinks. Simple, classic recipes are unbeatable if you're working with good ingredients and understand the techniques that will bring out the best in them.

A few supplies will come into play no matter which drinks you choose; keep these items on hand and you'll always be ready for a party.

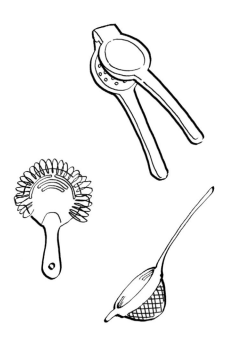

TOOLS

You could mix your cocktails in a bowl, measure your ingredients with teaspoons, and stir them with a fork, but part of the fun and the show of bartending is using the proper tools. The cheapest available versions of these items will do the trick. (Plus, once you get into home bartending, someone in your life will upgrade them for your birthday.)

Jiggers: Tom Cruise looked super hot in the movie *Cocktail*, flipping bottles and slinging ribbons of liquor into shakers. His drinks probably sucked, though. Good drinks are made with precise pours. As with baking a cake, a half ounce too much or too little can make a big difference in a small glass. A set of three stainless steel cocktail jiggers, with measurements ranging from ½ ounce to 2 ounces, are all you need to make any recipe.

Mixing Glass/Shaker: A two-part Boston shaker (one part metal tin, one part pint-size mixing glass) is inexpensive and versatile. See page 256 for our disaster-free shaking procedure.

Bar Spoon: Make sure it's long enough to reach all the way to the bottom of the mixing glass.

Juice Press: Fresh citrus juice makes cocktails shine. A citrus press squeezes the maximum juice out of your fruit while straining out pulp and seeds.

Strainer: A Hawthorne strainer fits perfectly over the top of the mixing glass and holds back the ice while you pour. The OXO version has a little raised lip that allows you to pour a drink very neatly. A julep strainer is like a perforated bowl with a little handle on it. It serves the same purpose (straining, ice holding). Which you use is a matter of preference, but you may find that one or the other fits best in your mixing glass or shaker. They're cheap and look cool–get both of them.

Fine-Mesh Strainer: This is not essential, but straining your mixed drink through a fine strainer will remove little bits of fruit and the small ice shards that dilute a drink as it sits.

GLASSWARE

A chilly gin martini, made with a dose of high-quality vermouth and garnished with a curl of fragrant lemon zest, will never taste as good without its proper glass. If you want to serve martinis and other cocktails, you'll need to pick up a few specialized glasses.

When choosing your glassware, be sure to pay attention to the volume of the glass as well as the design. There are some deceptively huge glasses out there. Filling them to the brim will get you in trouble; filled only partway, with a correctly measured drink, they'll look lame.

Martini (6 ounces): We prefer the traditional glass, shaped like a V.

Collins (12 to 13 ounces): If a gin and tonic looks good in the glasses you use for water, skip this one.

Coupe (5 to 6 ounces): The old-fashioned Champagne coupe has fallen out of favor for sparkling wine service, but has emerged as an elegant vessel for a drink served "up." A 5- to 6-ounce coupe is large enough to act as your martini glass, as well–with room to spare, if you like to garnish yours with a fat green olive.

Rocks (10 ounces): These should be wide enough to accommodate your new giant ice cubes (see page 255).

martini   collins   coupe

Rocks

THE SUPPORTING PLAYERS

These are the other things you'll need, all of which play an important role in making your drinks taste and look great.

Vermouth: Good vermouth is delicious, and it needs to be stored carefully to stay that way. (Forget the dusty bottle at the back of your parents' liquor cabinet–if you need to ask why, take a sip.) Buy smaller bottles and store leftovers in the refrigerator. If you have vacuum stoppers (you should, because they are cheap and great for storing an open bottle of wine), close the bottle with one of those. Properly stored, an open bottle of vermouth will last about a month. We recommend the Dolin label for dry vermouth and Carpano Antica Formula for sweet.

Bitters: Bitters provide a counterpoint to the sweet and sour notes in your drinks. The obscure barks, roots, and herbs that flavor these concoctions also add wonderful complexity to your cocktail recipes. Most classic cocktails call for specific bitters; changing these up is one way to create your own variations. The most common and useful brand to keep on hand is Angostura, which is spicy and a bit earthy. Regans' Orange Bitters No. 6 is great for a citrusy note. The many varieties of Fee Brothers bitters are fun to play with because each highlights a single ingredient. Most bitters will hold forever without refrigeration, but you may come across one that contains an ingredient that goes bad quickly. Check the label for storage directions.

Citrus Juice: Those bottles in the supermarket filled with pasteurized citrus juices? Leave them on the shelf. Over the years, they've given some beautiful classic cocktails an unfairly lousy reputation. Make yourself a daiquiri or a gimlet with fresh-squeezed juice and you'll see what we mean.

Simple Syrup: We use simple syrup (sugar dissolved in water) rather than straight sugar to sweeten our cocktails, as well as our iced tea and cold-brew coffee. Syrup incorporates more easily so you don't end up with crunchy crystals at the bottom of your drink. The recipe is simple, too: Combine equal parts sugar and boiling water in a container and stir to dissolve. The syrup holds forever– preferably in the fridge so little drips on the outside won't attract bugs.

ICE

No single ice cube will work for all your cocktail mixing and serving needs. Luckily, you can make all the ice you need using your home freezer and a bit of ingenuity.

Ice for Mixing: For drink mixing, as well as for tall iced drinks like a gin and tonic, any standard ice cube will do.

Ice for Serving: Smaller ice shapes, like those little crescents that come out of many home ice machines, fit compactly in a glass and have more surface area exposed. They will cool more quickly than a larger cube, but they will melt—and dilute—more quickly as well. This is great for a highball, like a whiskey and soda, where a bit of dilution is welcome. But for a carefully measured, nuanced cocktail or straight, unadulterated liquor on the rocks, you're going to want a big fat cube that won't weaken your drink so quickly. Most kitchen stores now carry inexpensive silicone ice trays that make big cubes and spheres, not to mention novelty shapes. (Chill your old-fashioned with the Death Star!)

Crushed Ice: If you want to make a Moscow mule or a mint julep, you're going to need crushed ice. (We find that almost any drink served over crushed ice during the dog days of summer will be gratefully received.) If you don't own an ice crusher, use a blender (be sure to drain the water from the ice before transferring to glasses), or put some cubes in a clean cloth napkin and smash away with a mallet or rolling pin.

Small Cubes

Large Cube

Crescent

Crushed

Techniques

The drink recipes in this book, and elsewhere, will instruct you to measure, stir, shake, and strain. Technique is the difference between a great cocktail and an indifferent one. Here's what you need to know.

Measuring: Whichever jiggers you use, be sure to figure out how to use them accurately. Some designs have a line that shows the correct measurements; others you fill right up to the rim. When you're measuring ½- to 2-ounce pours, a splash more or less makes a big difference.

One measurement that's never precise is the ubiquitous "dash" of bitters. It's a bit like a "pinch" of salt, in that it requires you to adjust a recipe to your taste. As a starting point, a dash refers to one swift, authoritative shake of a bitters bottle into your mixing glass. If you want real precision, look into Japanese dasher bottles, which will dispense a consistent dose each time.

Shaking: Shaking chills a drink, incorporates a bit of air, and dilutes it as the ice cubes chip and melt. Drinks made with citrus, egg whites, or dairy generally benefit from these effects. Also, shaking is fun. Using the two-part Boston shaker may seem intimidating, but it's actually pretty foolproof. You will master these steps in far less time than you spent learning to shuffle a deck of cards when you were twelve. Practice on your own using ice and water and keep a towel close at hand.

1. Measure your ingredients into the glass part of your shaker, then fill the glass about three-quarters full with ice.

2. Fit the metal shaker part over the top of the glass at a slight angle and bump the bottom of the tin with the heel of your hand to make a seal. You can check the seal by lifting the shaker a few inches off the counter, holding the metal part only, to make sure that the glass is stuck to the tin.

3. Flip the shaker so that the metal part is on the bottom. Shaking with the tin on the bottom keeps the opening facing your way so any stray drops will hit you and not your enraptured audience.

4. If you're worried about the glass flying away, keep one hand on the base of the glass and one on the base of the tin. If you want to play a hand of poker while you shake, hold the shaker tin with one hand, with your thumb and forefinger on the glass to keep it in place.

5. Shake vigorously for 10 to 15 seconds. The more you shake, the more diluted, aerated, and chilled (to a point) your drink will become. This is a matter of taste. You can adjust your shake time for each recipe as you discover your preferences.

6. Put the shaker on the counter, metal side down. Using the heel of your hand, break the seal by giving a firm tap on the metal

tin where it meets the side of the glass. Wiggle the glass free from the tin. It may take a bit of tapping and wiggling. Don't be too gentle; the thick-walled pint glass won't break easily.

7. Your drink is now ready to strain and serve.

Stirring: Drinks that are all or mostly liquor–like a martini, Manhattan, or Negroni–are generally stirred. The goal is to chill the drink while keeping it as clear and undiluted as possible. Your bar spoon, long and flat, was designed with this goal in mind. You can stir drinks in the glass part of your shaker, or in a larger vessel if you're mixing more than that glass can hold.

1. Fill the mixing glass about three-quarters of the way with ice and measure your ingredients onto the ice.

2. Slide the spoon down the inside wall of the glass. Stir by running the spoon around the wall of the glass, which will cause the ice to spin with a minimum of rattling and chipping. For most drinks, 30 seconds of stirring does a good job of chilling a drink with minimum dilution.

3. Your drink is now ready to strain and serve.

Straining: Your Hawthorne or julep strainer will separate the drink from the ice. For some cocktails, this may be all the straining you need. No one minds a bit of cloudiness and a few slivers of ice in a margarita.

Other drinks are more enjoyable when double-strained through a fine mesh to remove bits of fruit and ice that will dilute the drink and make it less pretty. When using a fine-mesh strainer, set it over the top of the drinking glass and strain the drink from the Hawthorne or julep strainer through the fine strainer into the glass.

MAKING A TWIST

There are a number of techniques out there for making fancy spiral twists. We prefer this method, which is not only the simplest, but delivers a fat, flavorful twist. Using organic fruit is a good idea, considering that conventional citrus fruit is exposed to pesticides and waxes, though you won't notice a difference in taste.

1. Rinse the fruit and dry gently.

2. Using a paring knife or peeler, cut a piece of rind about 1 inch wide and 1½ inches long, taking off as little of the white pith as possible.

3. Before garnishing, spritz the oils out of the twist by bending it in half, peel side down, over the surface of the drink. Then drop it in.

THE
FIVE
ESSENTIAL
COCKTAILS

THE FOLLOWING FIVE COCKTAILS are among the world's most beloved. Our bartenders sling them all night long and, when they're inventing their own drinks, these classic recipes provide inspiration and, often, a starting point. Alongside each of these quintessential cocktails we have included a variation from our restaurants. These cocktails swap ingredients but stay true to the essence of the originals.

Once you get the hang of tweaking classic recipes, you can invent your own drink. And then—the best part of being a mixologist—you get to name it.

Note: *The recipes in this chapter suggest one or two brands of each liquor used. These are starting points, not hard-and-fast rules. Feel free to experiment with the brands you find at a good liquor store.*

THE

MANHATTAN

Serves 1

2 ounces
RYE WHISKEY
(suggested: Old Overholt
or Rittenhouse)

1 ounce
SWEET VERMOUTH
(suggested: Carpano Antica Formula
or Dolin Rouge)

2 dashes
ANGOSTURA BITTERS

LEMON TWIST OR
COCKTAIL CHERRY,
for garnish

Interborough rivalries aside, the Manhattan is an essential cocktail. (The borough of Manhattan has its uses, too.) This is the cocktail most often called for at our bars, and it's the kind of simple, nothing-up-my-sleeve recipe that allows you to show off your new measuring and mixing skills. You can put your own spin on this drink by tweaking the amount and brand of vermouth and the bitters you use. If you opt for the traditional cocktail cherry, we recommend the insanely delicious maraschino cherries made by Luxardo in Italy. Those old waxy, neon-red things are strictly for Shirley Temples.

Chill your coupe or martini glass in the freezer or by filling it with ice and water while you mix the drink. Measure the rye, vermouth, and bitters into the glass of your shaker, then fill the glass about three-quarters full with ice. Stir swiftly with a cocktail spoon for 30 seconds. Double-strain into the chilled glass and garnish with a lemon twist or cherry.

The Saul Panzer

Serves 1

The Saul Panzer, named after the piano- and pinochle-playing detective who freelances for Nero Wolfe, has all the Manhattan's basic elements (rye whiskey, something bitter, something sweet), along with some exotic flair. China-China is a bittersweet French liqueur made from bitter orange peel, with notes of quinine and earthy gentian; maraschino liqueur has a pure, tart, floral cherry flavor.

Chill your coupe or martini glass in the freezer or by filling it with ice and water while you mix the drink. Measure the rye, China-China, vermouth, and maraschino into the glass of your shaker, then fill the glass about three-quarters full with ice. Stir swiftly with a cocktail spoon for 30 seconds. Double-strain into the chilled glass and garnish with a lemon twist or cherry.

2 ounces
RYE WHISKEY
(suggested: Rittenhouse or another 100-proof rye)

½ ounce
BIGALLET CHINA-CHINA

½ ounce
DRY VERMOUTH
(suggested: Dolin Dry)

¼ ounce
MARASCHINO LIQUEUR
(suggested: Luxardo)

LEMON TWIST OR COCKTAIL CHERRY,
for garnish

THE
NEGRONI

Serves 1

1½ ounces
LONDON DRY GIN
(suggested: Beefeater)

¾ ounce
CAMPARI

¾ ounce
SWEET VERMOUTH
(Carpano Antica Formula is best.
Dolin Rouge, although French,
would be good, too.)

ORANGE TWIST,
for garnish

The bitter-citrusy Negroni is a lovely before-dinner drink, but consider yourself warned: this drink is all liquor, so it will hit you hard. The Negroni is always made with Campari, but there are many other excellent bitter liqueurs in the world, and substituting them in this recipe is a great way to invent your own variation.

Like a martini, the Negroni is a drink that inspires many personal preferences. They can be served up, in a coupe or martini glass, or over ice in a rocks glass. Some people like a lot more gin; others prefer an equal ratio with the Campari. This is our recipe, which we generally serve in a rocks glass over a big cube of ice.

Chill your glass (coupe or martini glass if serving up, rocks glass if serving over ice) in the freezer or by filling it with ice and water while you mix the drink. Measure the gin, Campari, and vermouth into the glass of your shaker, then fill the glass about three-quarters full with ice. Stir swiftly with a cocktail spoon for 30 seconds. Strain into the chilled coupe or martini glass, or a rocks glass with ice, and garnish with an orange twist.

The Fox 8

Serves 1

We named this drink after a George Saunders story in which a precocious fox dreams of moving into a human home and becoming a member of the family. We like to think of Fox 8 lounging with his people friends and sipping this sophisticated take on a Negroni. Both the Salers and the Dolin Blanc provide herbaceous notes and mild sweetness, with a particular earthiness in the Salers that comes from gentian root.

Chill your rocks glass in the freezer or by filling it with ice and water while you mix the drink. Measure the gin, Salers, and vermouth into the glass of your shaker, then fill the glass about three-quarters full with ice. Stir swiftly with a cocktail spoon for 30 seconds to chill. Strain into a chilled rocks glass over a large cube of ice and garnish with an orange twist.

1 ounce
GIN
(suggested: Hendrick's)

1 ounce
SALERS APERITIF

1 ounce
DOLIN BLANC VERMOUTH

ORANGE TWIST,
for garnish

THE
GIN MARTINI

Serves 1

**3 ounces
GIN**
(suggested: Beefeater, Plymouth,
Bombay Sapphire)

**¼ ounce
VERMOUTH**
(suggested: Dolin Dry)

**GREEN OLIVE OR
LEMON TWIST,**
for garnish

If you like your martini dry, we'll happily make it for you with just a whisper of vermouth, but we take ours with the traditional proportions.

Chill your coupe or martini glass in the freezer or by filling it with ice and water while you mix the drink. Measure the gin and vermouth into the glass of your shaker, then fill the glass about three-quarters full with ice. Stir swiftly with a cocktail spoon for 30 seconds. Strain into the chilled glass and garnish with a green olive or lemon twist.

Variation: *Every gin and vermouth is made with a unique blend of aromatics, so the flavors in this drink can vary widely depending on which you choose. The vast selection of gins and vermouths from around the world should provide you with enough variations for many happy evenings.*

HOLD THE BOOZE

Some of us don't drink, but no one should miss out on the cocktail hour. When our customers ask us for a "virgin" cocktail, we begin with a few questions: In a coupe or over ice? Sweet or sour? How do you feel about fresh herbs? Bubbles or no?

As with a boozy drink, the elements need to be in balance. Start with the ratio you'd use for any sour cocktail: one part sweet and one part sour. For a 12-ounce glass, measure 1½ ounces of each into your cocktail shaker, over ice. Adjust this ratio depending on your ingredients—honey is sweeter than fruit purée; orange juice is not as sour as lemon. For more complexity, use two sweets and/or two sours to fill that 1½-ounce jigger. Top these with a dose of something bitter and something aromatic. Shake vigorously, then pour over ice or into a coupe. Top with something bubbly and garnish with something pretty.

Sweet: fruit purée or muddled ripe fruit, fruit preserves, jam, simple syrup, honey, agave syrup, maple syrup

Sour: citrus juice, mild vinegar (sherry, Banyuls, Champagne), sour cherry juice

Bitter: citrus zest, muddled cranberries, 100 percent pure cranberry juice, tea (black, green, matcha, Earl Grey—whatever, just brew it strong and chill before using)

Aromatic: chile flakes, jalapeño, cucumber, fresh herbs (basil, mint, tarragon, thyme, and rosemary are favorites), lavender, fresh ginger

Bubbly: soda water, tonic water, ginger beer, root beer, kombucha

THE

FRENCH 75

Serves 1

1 ounce
LONDON DRY GIN
(suggested: Beefeater)
or COGNAC
(suggested: Hine or Dudognon)

½ ounce
SIMPLE SYRUP
(see page 254)

½ ounce
LEMON JUICE

4 ounces
SPARKLING WINE

LEMON TWIST,
for garnish

This is a rare example of a cocktail that can be made with different spirits and still go by the same name. The oldest recipes call for Cognac, and that's the only way you'll get one in New Orleans, but French 75s made with gin have been around almost as long and are preferred by many. The gin-based version, with its bitter, herbal notes, might work better as an aperitif, while the sweetness of Cognac makes for a great after-dinner drink. Purists insist on making this drink with Champagne, and someone could claim that it tastes better, but it's awfully expensive. Prosecco or cava works just fine, and their cleaner profile allows the gin and citrus to be the stars.

Measure the gin or Cognac, simple syrup, and lemon juice into the glass of your shaker, then fill the glass about three-quarters full with ice. Shake a few times to mix, then strain into the flute. Top with the sparkling wine, then garnish with a lemon twist.

The Honeysuckle Rose

Serves 1

This French 75 variation isn't nearly as sweet as the Honeysuckle Rose that Fats Waller sang about, but honey, gin, and lemon make for a magical combination. Topping it with a rosé sparkler makes it pretty.

Measure the gin, lemon juice, and honey into the glass of your shaker, then fill the glass about three-quarters full with ice. Shake 8 to 10 times to mix, then strain into the flute. Top with the sparkling wine and garnish with a lemon twist.

1 ounce
DRY GIN
(suggested: Beefeater)

½ ounce
LEMON JUICE

¼ ounce
HONEY

3 ounces
SPARKLING ROSÉ WINE

LEMON TWIST,
for garnish

When I'm taking sips from your tasty lips
Seems the honey fairly drips
You're confection, goodness knows
Honeysuckle Rose

—FATS WALLER

THE
MARGARITA

Serves 1

LIME WEDGE AND
COARSE SALT,
for rim (optional)

2 ounces
BLANCO TEQUILA
(suggested: Espolòn or Milagro)

1 ounce
COINTREAU

1 ounce
LIME JUICE

LIME WEDGE,
for garnish

The margarita earned a bad reputation in the 1980s and
'90s when it spawned a whole category of drinks you likely
associate with the most shameful night of your beach
vacation. People are sometimes surprised that we make
them at all—and then, a minute later, surprised again by
what a fresh, well-balanced cocktail a margarita can be.

A margarita should be made with freshly squeezed
lime juice, good tequila (100 percent agave), and
Cointreau, a quality citrus liqueur that tastes much better
than the cheaper triple sec. The remaining options are the
same at our bistros as they are at the swim-up bar at an
all-inclusive resort: up or rocks, salt rim or not. Honestly?
You really can't go wrong.

Chill your glass (coupe or martini glass if serving
up, rocks glass if serving over ice) in the freezer or by
filling it with ice and water while you mix the drink.
If using a salt rim, rub the rim of your glass with a
lime wedge and dredge it in salt. Measure the tequila,
Cointreau, and lime juice into the glass of your
shaker, then fill the glass about three-quarters full
with ice. Shake vigorously for about 20 seconds. Strain
into the chilled coupe or martini glass, or into a rocks
glass with ice, and garnish with a lime wedge.

The Chespirito

Serves 1

The Chespirito, an homage to Roberto Gómez Bolaños, Mexico's renowned humorist, gets its sweetness from honey rather than Cointreau and adds a smoky note from mezcal, Mexico's other agave-based spirit.

Chill your rocks glass in the freezer or by filling it with ice and water while you mix the drink. Measure the tequila, mezcal, lemon juice, and honey into the glass of your shaker, then fill the glass about three-quarters full with ice. Shake vigorously for about 20 seconds. Strain into a rocks glass over ice. Garnish with a lemon wheel.

1 ounce
BLANCO TEQUILA
(suggested: Espolòn or Milagro)

1 ounce
MEZCAL
(suggested: Del Maguey Vida or Sombra Mezcal Joven)

1 ounce
LEMON JUICE

½ ounce
HONEY

LEMON WHEEL,
for garnish

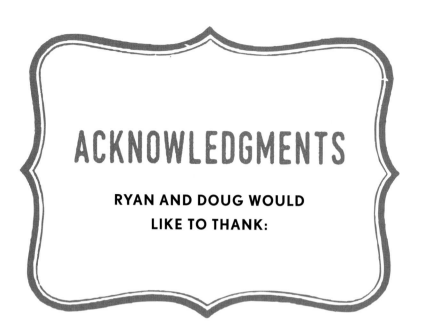

ACKNOWLEDGMENTS

RYAN AND DOUG WOULD LIKE TO THANK:

The staff, past and present, of Buttermilk Channel and French Louie. We didn't just invent this stuff; we built it with you. Having you in our lives has been the most fun and satisfying part of the whole journey.

The chefs: Ian Alvarez, Jon Check, Justin Fulton, and Chris Norton, for the long hot hours and for their many contributions to this book.

The pastry chefs: Yoko Ueno, Jennie Muoio, Krysta Buckley, and Jensen Donaldson, for the early mornings in freezing/sweltering basement kitchens and for the happy endings to so many meals.

Jennifer Nelson, for running the show and keeping it classy, and for your beautiful hospitality.

Ellen Simpson, for leading with empathy and humor, and for all the "y'alls."

Heather Ehmer, for bringing kindness, companionship, and traffic control to countless brunches.

Joseph Foglia, for a very handsome restaurant.

David Black, for your friendship, advocacy, inspiration, and for bringing publishing lunches to Boerum Hill.

The talented and delightful team at Grand Central Life & Style: Karen Murgolo, for your faith in us and for knowing when to reel us in; Brittany McInerney, for your sharp eye and good humor; and to Kallie Shimek, Karen Wise, Lisa Forde, and everyone who helped them and us to bring this book to life.

Laura Palese, for the stunning design.

Owen Brozman, for showing everyone what these recipes are supposed to look like, and for Louie.

Laura Tucker, for whipping us into shape.

OUR ARMY OF
RECIPE TESTERS

Liz Barclay, Suzanne Lenzer, and **Andie McMahon,** for the beautiful photographs.

Jane Lerner, for essential and timely editorial advice.

Vito Giallo, for inviting us into your beautiful home and allowing us to plunder your treasures.

Mike Mihalko and **Main Street Meats,** for the birds and beasts.

Jon Wilson and **Snug Harbor Heritage Farm,** for the veggies.

Kathleen Hackett
For getting us started.

Susanna Einstein + David Zimmerman
For simmering all the stocks.

Chrissann and Mike Gasparro
For not floundering the flounder.

Victoria Doyle
Our Green Goddess.

Sarah Goodyear and Laura Conaway
Yes whey can!
(Thanks for tasting, Nathaniel.)

Richard Sears
Turn up for turnips.

Sophie Lam
For picture-perfect cornbread.

Allison Sharp
For frying chicken, just in time.

Ellen Simpson
Con-spatula-tions on your perfect pancakes.

Phil Marriott + Susannah Taylor
Aioli you one.

Michal "General Custard" Shelkowitz
For the pro tips.

Jennifer Nelson
For cocktails and bar wisdom.

Geoff Woodcock
For averting a Bloody Mary disaster.

Anna Rak
Dziękuję ci za profiteroles.

Katie Wexler and Sean Hutchinson
The sun's a ball of butter, and your favorite mussels are, too.

Tricia and Jeffrey Rosen
For being unafraid to improvise.

Alexa Karstaedt
For the chopped livah.

Rebecca Traister and Darius Wadia
For taking time out from saving the world to roast duck legs.

Jane Lerner
For popping our popovers.

Anthony DiRenzo
El rey de la salchicha.

John Greenberg and Robert Zumwalt
For testing the most recipes.
You win.

INDEX

A-B-C Grilled Cheese, 202
Aioli, 4
Ancho Chile Marinade, Slow-Roasted Pork Spare Ribs with, 143
Ancho Chile Purée, 5
anchovies
    Anchovy Frites, 80
    Braised Short Ribs with Fried Lemon & Anchovy Mash, 144
    Lamb Blade Chops with Charred Sugar Snap Peas & Warm Anchovy Vinaigrette, 148
    in Lamb Club Sandwich, 154
    Leafy Greens with Toasted Bread Crumbs & Anchovy Vinaigrette, 52
apples
    in A-B-C Grilled Cheese, 202
    in Seared Scallops with Brussels Sprouts & Cider Brown Butter, 94
Apple Butter, 20
    Buckwheat Crêpes with Ricotta &, 190
Asparagus Soup with Toasted Almonds, Chilled White, 62
avocados
    in Green Goddess Salad, 42
    in Summer Sugar Snap Pea Salad, 50

bacon
    in A-B-C Grilled Cheese, 202
    in BBQ Oysters, 76
    in Green Goddess Salad, 42
Bananas Foster Profiteroles, 238
Banyuls Vinaigrette, Snug Harbor Greens with Torn Herbs &, 46
BBQ Oysters, 76
Béarnaise Sauce, 9
    in Eggs Louie, 195
    in Warm Lobster Cocktail, 85
beef. See also steak

Boeuf Bourguignon "à la Minute," 150
    Braised Short Ribs with Fried Lemon & Anchovy Mash, 144
    dry-aged, about, 159–60
    Short Rib Hash, 211
    Steak Frites, 156
    Steak Tartare, 125
Beet Hummus, Salt-Roasted, 58
Benton's Ham-Wrapped Trout with Mustardy Mustard Greens, 106
Blackberry Jam, 25
Black Olive Salt, 23
Black Pepper Fig Conserve, 22
Bloody Mary, 217
Bloody Mary bar, 212–15
    garnishes and add-ins, 214–15
    salt rims, 215
    setting the table, 215
    spirits, 212, 214
Blueberry Jam, 25
blue cheese, 175
    in Green Goddess Salad, 42
Bluefish, Grilled, with Cranberry Bean & Linguiça Stew, 100
Boeuf Bourguignon "à la Minute," 150
Bordelaise Sauce, 6
Braised Lamb Neck with Spring Peas, Omelet & Pistou, 140
Braised Short Ribs with Fried Lemon & Anchovy Mash, 144
braising meat, tips for, 147
Bread & Butter Pickles, 26
Breakfast Sausage, 207
Brussels Sprouts & Cider Brown Butter, Seared Scallops with, 94
Buckwheat Crêpes with Ricotta & Apple Butter, 190
Buttermilk Biscuits, 208
    in Eggs Huntington, 194

Buttermilk Cake, Lemon-Poppy, 232
Buttermilk Fried Chicken with Cheddar Waffles & Balsamic-Spiked Maple Syrup, 128
Buttermilk Ricotta, 14
    in Buckwheat Crêpes with Ricotta & Apple Butter, 190
    in Delicata Squash Tart, 228

Cake, Lemon-Poppy Buttermilk, 232
Capers, Fried, 30
Caramelized Chicken Jus, 18
carrots
    in Boeuf Bourguignon "à la Minute," 150
    Carrots Cooked in Whey, 15
    in Jardinière Pickles, 28
Cast-Iron Roasted Chicken with Beluga Lentils, Sunchokes & Walnut Vinaigrette, 126
cauliflower
    Cauliflower & Leek Soup with Dill, Scallion & Caraway Crème Fraîche, 57
    Chickpea Socca & Sunny-Side Up Eggs with Mixed Grains & Cauliflower, 187
    in Flounder Grenobloise, 110
    in Jardinière Pickles, 28
cheese
    about, 173–75
    A-B-C Grilled Cheese, 202
    in Gougères, 226
    selection tips, 173–75
    serving tips, 174
    Tarte au Fromage with Huckleberry & Lime, 242
cherries, in Summer Sugar Snap Pea Salad, 50
Cherry Pepper Jelly, Chicory Coffee-Rubbed Quail Kebabs with, 122
cherry peppers, pickled
    in Cornbread with Chile-Lime Butter, 230
    Narragansett Steamed Mussels with Cherry Peppers, Basil & Olives, 93
    in Parsley-Crusted Hake with Summer Beans, 108
Chespirito, the, 270
chicken

Buttermilk Fried Chicken with Cheddar Waffles & Balsamic-Spiked Maple Syrup, 128

Caramelized Chicken Jus, 18

Cast-Iron Roasted Chicken with Beluga Lentils, Sunchokes & Walnut Vinaigrette, 126

Chicken Liver Pâté, 124

Chicken Stock, 17

Cordon Bleu, 204

Chickpea Socca & Sunny-Side Up Eggs with Mixed Grains & Cauliflower, 187

Chicory Coffee-Rubbed Quail Kebabs with Cherry Pepper Jelly, 122

Chile-Lime Butter, Cornbread with, 230

Chilled East Beach Blonde Oysters with Grapefruit Mignonette, 70

Chilled Heirloom Tomato Soup with Torn Bread Croutons, 60

Chilled White Asparagus Soup with Toasted Almonds, 62

Chocolate Pots de Crème with Orange Crème Fraîche, 240

Clams, Portuguese-Style Pork &, 112

cocktails. *See also* Bloody Mary bar; home bar, setting up

about, 248

Bloody Mary, 217

The Chespirito, 270

Corpse Reviver No. 2, 216

The Fox 8, 263

The French 75, 267

The Gin Martini, 264

The Honeysuckle Rose, 268

The Manhattan, 260

The Margarita, 269

The Negroni, 262

The Saul Panzer, 261

Cordon Bleu, 204

Cornbread with Chile-Lime Butter, 230

Corpse Reviver No. 2, 216

crab(meat)

Crispy Skate Wing with Crab Bisque & Dirty Rice, 96

in Eggs Louie, 195

in Oysters Bienville, 78

Cranberry Bean & Linguiça Stew, Grilled Bluefish with, 100

crêpes, 187, 190

Crispy Skate Wing with Crab Bisque & Dirty Rice, 96

croissants, in Eggs Louie, 195

Cured Steelhead Trout Scramble, 201

Cured Steelhead Trout with Hash Browns & Lemon-Caper Crème Fraîche, 196

Delicata Squash Tart, 228

desserts

Bananas Foster Profiteroles, 238

Chocolate Pots de Crème with Orange Crème Fraîche, 240

Lemon-Poppy Buttermilk Cake, 232

Pineapple Tarte Tatin with Toasted Coconut Ice Cream, 234

Rum Raisin Torte, 237

Tarte au Fromage with Huckleberry & Lime, 242

Dill Pickles, 29

Dinde au Vin (Turkey Braised in Red Wine with Pork Belly & Mushrooms), 152

dining room, setting the stage, 166–67

Dirty Rice, Crispy Skate Wing with Crab Bisque &, 96

duck

Duck Breast au Poivre Blood Orange Marmalade & Baby Turnip Confit, 138

Duck Jus, 19

Duck Meatloaf, 134

Roast Duck Legs Allard with Castelvetrano Olives, Fennel Pollen & Duck Jus, 136

Dulse Butter & Rye Ficelle, Smoked Sardines with, 82

eggs

Chickpea Socca & Sunny-Side Up Eggs with Mixed Grains & Cauliflower, 187

Cured Steelhead Trout Scramble, 201

Eggs Huntington, 194

Eggs Louie, 195

in "Leftovers" Frittata, 199

Mushroom & Goat Cheese Scramble, 200

Pipérade & Merguez Scramble, 201

in Short Rib Hash, 211

Eggs Benedict, 192

endive

Grapefruit & Endive Salad, 203

in Green Goddess Salad, 42

Escarole, Radicchio, Fennel & Grape Salad, 51

espelette pepper, in Warm Lobster Cocktail, 85

fennel

Escarole, Radicchio, Fennel & Grape Salad, 51

in Jardinière Pickles, 28

Fig Conserve, Black Pepper, 22

fish and seafood. *See also* mussels; oysters

about, 66

Anchovy Frites, 80

Benton's Ham-Wrapped Trout with Mustardy Mustard Greens, 106

Crispy Skate Wing with Crab Bisque & Dirty Rice, 96

Flounder Grenobloise, 110

Grilled Bluefish with Cranberry Bean & Linguiça Stew, 100

Grilled Whole Porgy with Green Tomato Sauce Vierge, 104

Parsley-Crusted Hake with Summer Beans, 108

Portuguese-Style Pork & Clams, 112

Seared Scallops with Brussels Sprouts & Cider Brown Butter, 94

shopping tips, 99

Smoked Sardines with Dulse Butter & Rye Ficelle, 82

storage tips, 102–3

Warm Lobster Cocktail, 85

Flounder Grenobloise, 110

Fox 8, the, 263

French Fries (Pommes Frites), 164

French Toast, Pecan Pie, 182

French 75, the, 267

Fried Capers, 30

Fried Chicken with Cheddar Waffles & Balsamic-Spiked Maple Syrup, Buttermilk, 128

fries (frites)

Anchovy Frites, 80

Pommes Frites (French Fries), 164

Frittata, "Leftovers," 199

Gin Martini, the, 264

goat cheese

in Grits, 210

Mushroom & Goat Cheese Scramble, 200

goat cheese (*cont.*)

   in Tarte au Fromage with
      Huckleberry & Lime, 242

Gougères, 226

grapefruit

   Chilled East Beach Blonde Oysters
      with Grapefruit Mignonette, 70

   Grapefruit & Endive Salad,
      203

grapes

   Escarole, Radicchio, Fennel & Grape
      Salad, 51

   Vinegar Roasted Grapes, 175

Green Goddess Salad, 42

green tomatoes

   Grilled Whole Porgy with Green
      Tomato Sauce Vierge, 104

   in Jardinière Pickles, 28

Grenobloise, Flounder, 110

Grilled Bluefish with Cranberry Bean &
   Linguiça Stew, 100

Grilled Cheese, A-B-C, 202

Grilled Whole Porgy with Green
   Tomato Sauce Vierge, 104

Grits, 210

Hake, Parsley-Crusted, with Summer
   Beans, 108

ham

   Benton's Ham-Wrapped Trout with
      Mustardy Mustard Greens,
      106

   in Cordon Bleu, 204

   in Eggs Huntington, 194

Hollandaise Sauce, 8

   in Eggs Huntington, 194

home bar, setting up, 252–57

   glassware, 253

   ice, 255

   supporting players, 254

   techniques, 256–57

   tools, 252–53

Honeysuckle Rose, the, 268

Huckleberry Jam, 24

Hummus, Salt-Roasted Beet, 58

I-A Sauce, 12

Iceberg Wedge with Citrus French
   Dressing, Tarragon & Pickled
   Mustard Seeds, 48

Ice Cream, Pineapple Tarte Tatin with
   Toasted Coconut, 234

jams, 24, 25

Jardinière Pickles, 28

kale

   in Grilled Bluefish with Cranberry
      Bean & Linguiça Stew, 100

   in Portuguese-Style Pork & Clams, 112

Kebabs, Chicory Coffee-Rubbed Quail,
   with Cherry Pepper Jelly, 122

lamb

   Braised Lamb Neck with Spring
      Peas, Omelet & Pistou, 140

   Lamb Blade Chops with Charred
      Sugar Snap Peas & Warm
      Anchovy Vinaigrette, 148

   Lamb Club Sandwich, 154

Leafy Greens with Toasted Bread
   Crumbs & Anchovy Vinaigrette, 52

"Leftovers" Frittata, 199

Lemon-Caper Crème Fraîche, Cured
   Steelhead Trout with Hash
   Browns &, 196

Lemon-Poppy Buttermilk Cake, 232

lentils

   Cast-Iron Roasted Chicken with
      Beluga Lentils, Sunchokes &
      Walnut Vinaigrette, 126

   Lentil & Walnut Pâté, 56

lettuce, cleaning tips, 44–45

lights (lighting), 166–67

linguiça

   Grilled Bluefish with Cranberry
      Bean & Linguiça Stew, 100

   in Portuguese-Style Pork & Clams, 112

Lobster Cocktail, Warm, 85

Maître d'Hôtel Butter, 163

Manhattan, the, 260

Margarita, the, 269

Meatloaf, Duck, 134

Mornay Sauce, in Cordon Bleu, 204

Mushroom & Goat Cheese Scramble,
   200

mushrooms

   Boeuf Bourguignon "à la Minute," 150

   Dinde au Vin (Turkey Braised in
      Red Wine with Pork Belly &
      Mushrooms), 152

   Mushroom & Goat Cheese
      Scramble, 200

   in Oysters Bienville, 78

music, setting the stage, 167

mussels

   Mussels Normande, 89

   Mussels Pipérade, 90

   Narragansett Steamed Mussels with
      Cherry Peppers, Basil & Olives,
      93

Mustard Greens, Benton's Ham-Wrapped
   Trout with Mustardy, 106

Mustard Seeds. *See* Pickled Mustard
   Seeds

Narragansett Steamed Mussels with
   Cherry Peppers, Basil & Olives, 93

Negroni, the, 262

Normande, Mussels, 89

nuts, toasting tips, 49

Oven-Dried Tomatoes, 16

   in Iceberg Wedge with Citrus French
      Dressing, Tarragon & Pickled
      Mustard Seeds, 48

oysters

   about, 73

   BBQ Oysters, 76

   Chilled East Beach Blonde Oysters
      with Grapefruit Mignonette, 70

   Oysters Bienville, 78

   Oysters with Saltines, 74

Pancakes, 184

pantry staples, 21

Parsley-Crusted Hake with Summer
   Beans, 108

Parsley Pistou, 10

pâtés, 56, 124

Pecan Pie French Toast, 182

Pickled Mustard Seeds, 31

   Iceberg Wedge with Citrus French
      Dressing, Tarragon &, 48

pickles, 26, 28, 29

Pie Dough, 227

Pineapple Tarte Tatin with Toasted
   Coconut Ice Cream, 234

Pipérade, Mussels, 90

Pipérade & Merguez Scramble, 201

Pommes Frites (French Fries), 164

Popovers with Honey & Sea Salt, 224

Porgy, Grilled Whole, with Green
   Tomato Sauce Vierge, 104

pork. *See also* bacon; ham

   in Breakfast Sausage, 207

Portuguese-Style Pork & Clams, 112
Slow-Roasted Pork Spare Ribs with
Ancho Chile Marinade, 143
Turkey Braised in Red Wine with Pork
Belly & Mushrooms, 152
Portuguese-Style Pork & Clams, 112
potatoes
Cured Steelhead Trout with Hash
Browns & Lemon-Caper Crème
Fraîche, 196
Pommes Frites (French Fries), 164
in Short Rib Hash, 211
Profiteroles, Bananas Foster, 238

Quail Kebabs with Cherry Pepper Jelly,
Chicory Coffee-Rubbed, 122

Radicchio, Escarole, Fennel & Grape
Salad, 51
Radishes with Butter & Black Olive
Salt, 54
Raspberry Jam, 25
ricotta. See Buttermilk Ricotta
Roast Duck Legs Allard with
Castelvetrano Olives, Fennel
Pollen & Duck Jus, 136
Roasted Chicken, Cast-Iron, with
Beluga Lentils, Sunchokes &
Walnut Vinaigrette, 126
Rum Raisin Torte, 237

salads
about, 38
Escarole, Radicchio, Fennel & Grape
Salad, 51
Grapefruit & Endive Salad, 203
Green Goddess Salad, 42
Iceberg Wedge with Citrus French
Dressing, Tarragon & Pickled
Mustard Seeds, 48
Leafy Greens with Toasted Bread
Crumbs & Anchovy Vinaigrette, 52
Snug Harbor Greens with Torn
Herbs & Banyuls Vinaigrette, 46
Summer Sugar Snap Pea Salad, 50
salad spinners, 44–45
salt
about, xi, 32–33
measuring and substituting, 33
types of, 33
Salt-Roasted Beet Hummus, 58
sandwiches, 154, 202

Sardines, Smoked, with Dulse Butter &
Rye Ficelle, 82
Sauce Gribiche, String Beans with, 55
Saul Panzer, the, 261
Scallops, Seared, with Brussels Sprouts &
Cider Brown Butter, 94
Scrambles, 200, 201
seafood. See fish and seafood
Seared Scallops with Brussels Sprouts &
Cider Brown Butter, 94
Short Rib Hash, 211
Skate Wing, Crispy, with Crab Bisque &
Dirty Rice, 96
Slow-Roasted Pork Spare Ribs with
Ancho Chile Marinade, 143
Smoked Sardines with Dulse Butter &
Rye Ficelle, 82
Snug Harbor Greens with Torn Herbs &
Banyuls Vinaigrette, 46
Socca, Chickpea, & Sunny-Side Up
Eggs with Mixed Grains &
Cauliflower, 187
soups
Cauliflower & Leek Soup with Dill,
Scallion & Caraway Crème
Fraîche, 57
Chilled Heirloom Tomato Soup with
Torn Bread Croutons, 60
Chilled White Asparagus Soup with
Toasted Almonds, 62
Squash Tart, Delicata, 228
steak
cooking for a party, 162
cooking methods, 161
cooking tips, 160
determining doneness, 161
selection tips, 158–59
shopping tips, 158
Steak Frites, 156
Steak Tartare, 125
Stock, Chicken, 17
Strawberry Jam, 25
string beans
in Jardinière Pickles, 28
String Beans with Sauce
Gribiche, 55
sugar snap peas
Lamb Blade Chops with Charred
Sugar Snap Peas & Warm
Anchovy Vinaigrette, 148
Summer Sugar Snap Pea Salad, 50

Summer Beans, Parsley-Crusted Hake
with, 108
Summer Sugar Snap Pea Salad, 50
Sunchokes & Walnut Vinaigrette, Cast-
Iron Roasted Chicken with Beluga
Lentils, 126

Tartare, Steak, 125
tarts
Delicata Squash Tart, 228
Pineapple Tarte Tatin with Toasted
Coconut Ice Cream, 234
Rum Raisin Torte, 237
Tarte au Fromage with Huckleberry &
Lime, 242
temperature of the room, 167
Toasted Coconut Ice Cream, Pineapple
Tarte Tatin with, 234
tomatoes. See also green tomatoes;
Oven-Dried Tomatoes
Chilled Heirloom Tomato Soup with
Torn Bread Croutons, 60
Tomato Concassé, 105
trout
Benton's Ham-Wrapped Trout with
Mustardy Mustard Greens, 106
Cured Steelhead Trout Scramble,
201
Cured Steelhead Trout with Hash
Browns & Lemon-Caper Crème
Fraîche, 196
Turkey Braised in Red Wine with Pork
Belly & Mushrooms (Dinde au
Vin), 152
twists, making, 257

Vinegar Roasted Grapes, 175

Waffles & Balsamic-Spiked Maple
Syrup, Buttermilk Fried Chicken
with Cheddar, 128
Walnut & Lentil Pâté, 56
Walnut Vinaigrette, Cast-Iron Roasted
Chicken with Beluga Lentils,
Sunchokes &, 126
Warm Lobster Cocktail, 85
whey, 15
Whey Brine, 15
wine
about, 169–71
cheese pairings, 174
food combinations to avoid, 171

ABOUT THE AUTHORS

RYAN ANGULO was born and raised in Rhode Island, where he attended the Culinary Arts Program at Johnson & Wales University. Ryan has traveled throughout the United States, working at restaurants in Rhode Island, California, Atlanta, New Orleans, Hawaii, and New York. With Doug Crowell, he opened Buttermilk Channel as its executive chef in 2008 and, in 2014, he opened French Louie as chef and co-owner. His take on American cuisine has been featured in the *New York Times*, *Bon Appétit*, *Time Out New York*, and *Food & Wine*, and on the Food Network.

DOUG CROWELL is a native New Yorker and a graduate of the Culinary Institute of America. He worked in the kitchens at a number of restaurants in Boston and New York, including Picholine and La Grenouille, before moving to the front of the house to run several of Manhattan's largest and most popular dining rooms. In 2008, he opened Buttermilk Channel, followed by French Louie in 2014.